leaves

for the
birds

MOVEMENTS
FOR
JUSTICE

MARJORIE BEAUCAGE

KEGEDONCE PRESS, 2023

Published by Kegedonce Press
11 Park Road, Neyaashiinigmiing, ON N0H 2T0
Administration Office/Book Orders: P.O. Box 517, Owen Sound, ON N4K 5R1
www.kegedonce.com

Art Direction: Kateri Akiwenzie-Damm
Cover artwork: "Crow and Me" by Susan Sacobie
Inside artwork and photos: Marjorie Beaucage
Author's photo: Kenton Doupe (La Moisson)
Design: Chantal Lalonde Design
Printed in Canada by Trico Packaging & Print Solutions

Library and Archives Canada Cataloguing in Publication

Title: leave some for the birds : movements for justice / Marjorie Beaucage.
Names: Beaucage, Marjorie, author.
Description: Poems.
Identifiers: Canadiana 20230174310 | ISBN 9781928120360 (softcover)
Classification: LCC PS8603.E2525 L43 2023 | DDC C811/.6—dc23

For Customer Service/Orders
Tel 1–800–591–6250 Fax 1–800–591–6251
100 Armstrong Ave. Georgetown, ON L7G 5S4
Email: orders@litdistco.ca

We acknowledge the support of the Canada Council for the Arts which last year
invested $20.1 million in writing and publishing throughout Canada.

Canada Council   Conseil des arts
for the Arts   du Canada

We would like to acknowledge funding support from the Ontario Arts Council,
an agency of the Government of Ontario.

ONTARIO ARTS COUNCIL
CONSEIL DES ARTS DE L'ONTARIO

an Ontario government agency
un organisme du gouvernement de l'Ontario

To the future ancestors and dreamers.

Table of Contents

Remnants

Rummaging through the remnants of my life. Again. Looking for pathways to the forgotten ones. Calling me home. Drawing me in. To a place of knowing. Tapping in. Tuning out the crackling of old tapes. Reigniting the flame of my truth. If there are ashes here, there must have been fire once. Fire needs kindling kind links kind hands to ignite the spark into wisps of flame. Gentle breaths to nurture into loving embrace. Fire cannot burn hot alone in this cold cold world. Fire me fire me up. Fire me down. Fire me all around until I become holy ash to be scattered. Returning to feed you.

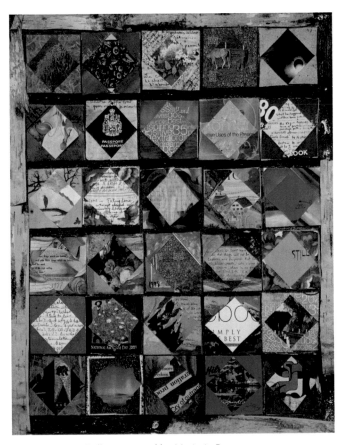

Collage created by Marjorie Beaucage.
Photo by Barbara Reimer.

Prologue

Some part of me has always heard the music of a greater dance.

I have moved and been moved throughout my life. I am a mover, on pilgrimage. Seeking my purpose, making my way, choosing my paths, trailblazing where a path did not exist.

Memories. What I re-member. What is real: possible histories, dreams, fantasies? Still, memories are stepping stones from times past. As I sift through my past lives and uncover truths, lessons, confessions, insights gaining an understanding who I am, what have I learned?

To recollect is to re-enter and transform.

Each of us has a value perspective, an "authority" within. It is unique and personal. Often it is not conscious or conceptual. It is in our gut influencing our actions in "crunch" situations.

I was born with a why in my mouth, questioning questioning questioning.

I recognize the way we order and structure our lives is our own making. There are many contradictions within systems that need to be confronted as our human realities change. In seeing the contradictions, I am forced to seek alternatives, not just adapt to what is. Refusing to accept structures that no longer serve. Seeking change. Not playing according to old rules when a whole new way is needed. Refusing to be caught by guilt, apathy or despair.

What is the shape of the new order? Dreaming and wooing new combinations for justice making. Forming new relations. Being imaginative, irrational, spontaneous, beyond the pragmatic and realistic. Losing my bonds. Sunsets blessing me, moonbeams and northern lights dancing in my soul. Midwife to my Self.

These movements of my life are based on seven decades of living and seeking justice as a Two Spirit Michif woman. I have been part of many social movements in my life, and in the last forty years I have expressed my search for justice as an artivist, using art and story medicine to create social change.

I began writing my life in 2016 when I was accepted to the Santa Fe Art Institute for a three-month Equal Justice Artist residency. I spent this time going through boxes of old journals and notes that spanned my life of working creating loving and fighting for justice. What can I pass on to future activists and dreamers?

Poems floated through my journals. I have never shared them or read them out loud. While in New Mexico, I explored spoken word and the incredible vulnerability of laying bare from the inside out. I am grateful to Israel Lopez for opening this door of truth saying for me. On my 70th birthday I had a ceremony to burn my journals, to let it all go, keeping the lessons learned and bits of beauty to create newness.

Time and space are constructions. This story is not linear. I came to understand the movements of my life as currents running through me, deep underground streams, unconscious still waters, dammed up tributaries, spring melts. Childhood, spirituality, woman-ness, revolution, creation were sources sustaining me as I navigated my place and purpose in life.

My life journey has taken me from New York City to Labrador to the Philippines and China. Each 'movement' of my life has been an encounter with the injustices of colonialism and poverty, and as I collected these stories together, I saw themes that my younger activist self could have learned from. Especially the need to sustain and heal one's spirit in a world that has too often undervalued difference.

I have also reflected on the impact of the feminist movement on Indigenous women and my relations with women as a part of my journey. As a filmmaker and storyteller I have examined institutional racism in its many forms and their impact on me. It is time to be seen and heard.

Marjorie (eldest) and her siblings. Photo by Auntie Alice.

Childhood

"Childhood is a place as well as a time."

—May Sarton

Seeds on the forest floor

Li bleuets tout ronds toute murs toute bleu.
          Blueberries so round so ripe so blue.
    Prends les pas toutes ma p'tite
          Don't take them all my girl
prends les pas toutes
          don't take them all
laisse zen pour lis oiseaux
          leave some for the birds.
O lis oiseaux.
          O the birds.
J'appris leur language dans le bois
          I learned their language in the bush
leurs chuchottements leurs chansons
          their twitterings their songs
leurs cantiques
          their hymns
de remerciement.
          of thanksgiving.
Oublie pas ma p'tite.
          Don't forget my girl.
Oublie pas d'où sa vient.
          Don't forget where they come from.
je me souviens mémère je me souviens.
          I remember grandma, I remember.

I am winter born

I am winter born. The howling winter wind swallowed my birth cry in my grand-mother's house. The snow-laden branches of the evergreens still shelter the hardy birds. The frozen moon aura on a cold and bitter night blessed me. These are my first teachers.

I am night born. Silent night. Stillness. Dark. Desiring light and the kindling of fires to create warmth, drawing everyone closer.

My parents were first cousins. This was not supposed to happen. I already had a half-brother older than me though I did not know he was my brother until I was an adult. Family secrets.

Fragments

Lying in a meadow
in last year's tall hay, still brown
flat on my stomach eye level
with sweet wild strawberries
us kids like gophers
popping up
trying to see where the others were.

Thunderstorms where clouds rolled in fast
green with hail
Sunday afternoon baseball tournaments
chasing foul balls for ice cream cones
where my dad was the ump
steeeee-rike.

And I could legitimately stand behind the wire at home plate
and yell "Kill the ump!"
What has been taken?
No father-daughter here.
What is it like to be fathered?
Protected, safe and secure?
Is there a place to put my hurt?

Early Teachers and Influences

"Learn to do by doing."

—4-H motto

My first experience of popular education was in 4-H where my mom and aunties were the teachers, passing on their knowledge and skills. A movement where local leadership was recognized. My first public speaking gig: "Accidents don't just happen. They are caused." Already wanting people to take responsibility for their actions. The world of 4-H fairs, gardens and sewing clubs opened a world outside of home.

Every day, I got up early for morning mass and delivered the Winnipeg Free Press to my twelve customers before school. Paper money for a left-handed baseball glove or a fancy pencil case or binder for school. Breakfast of porridge or Red River cereal with cinnamon, sometimes raisins and toast from homemade bread. We came home at lunch for hearty soups of peas, barley, vegetables with broths from soup bones. Our two-room schoolhouse was just across the tracks. Our only link to the outside world was the train that came in every night and dropped off supplies and newspapers. Standing on the platform I wondered who and where these people were going.

School was a reprieve from chores and kids. A place to rest and dream. I was an avid reader, escaping into imagination. Not much of a library, the Lives of the Saints became my role models. "Striving for perfection!" I wanted to be a saint when I grew up!

I was taught by the Sisters of St Joseph from Quebec. L'histoire du Canada was quite different than what I learned later in English. I had to unlearn a lot of things.

"Perdre sa langue c'est perdre sa foi…" The English inspector was the devil incarnate; he had a Masonic ring. When he gave us a spelling test, he gave us this sentence: "The children played happily in the yard." I thought 'Happily' was an English game and it was unfair to use a game we did not know!

As a kid, I remember being told to snap out of it, quit daydreaming, get your nose out of that book. Look after the kids. Do this. Do that. I remember a teacher saying 'tu fausses,' to just mouth the words when I was singing. And my imaginary underworld glazed sea floor was not good enough, yet I was so proud of it and had worked on it for a long time. I cannot draw. Being left-handed was not a gift. Yet somehow my creativity survived. I insisted on being different and unique, maybe too much, that there was no possible way for me to feel I belonged anywhere.

Often feeling resentful and angry, I resisted authority and was afraid to partake. I was not supposed to have desires, to want things.

I was the oldest of twelve siblings and had the responsibility to help with chores and kids, hauling water from the well, emptying slop pails, changing diapers, watching the kids outside, rows and rows of weeding and harvesting the garden, preparing meals and dishes. So many dishes.

Feeling alone in the midst of it all. Having no words to break through the suffering and poverty I saw around me. Seeing my mother pregnant over and over, worrying. Coming home from school and wondering where the furniture went – repossessed for a missed payment. Who would take away a washing machine from a family with so many kids? The worst was being sent to the beer parlor to get my dad.

Bush camp

Popcorn
a large white enamel dishpan full!
Bush camp break-up at Moose Lake
sitting on the top bunk
dreaming of faraway places.
Spring in the air.
Jack pine wafting new green.
Wind whispering through the pines
imagining what the ocean sounds like
though I have never seen one.

My beloved forest.
The longest I ever stayed anywhere.
We had to move from this place
where my dad and uncles harvested the forest
with their little sawmill operation making two by fours
and firewood
because the government
gave all the cutting rights to a big pulp mill in Sprague.
My homeland becoming a provincial forest
mostly a tree farm now.
My first sense of social injustice.
Displaced.

In movement ever since.

Popcorn. Again.
I was twelve
on a runaway Sunday afternoon
with my cousin Dolores and her boyfriend.
Why did she bring me along
crossing the USA border to Roseau Minnesota?

A dark theatre with soft seats and popcorn.
Old Yeller in large screen technicolour splendor.
Until then, I had only seen old black and white westerns like
Gene Autry, the *Lone Ranger and Zorro*
sitting on Coke boxes in the community hall.
In high school, I remember
High Noon and *Twelve Angry Men*
standing up for what you believe
no matter what.

The Seven Works of Mercy

Works of Mercy: a concept from Acts of the Apostles and living precepts of the Catholic Worker Movement which has influenced my being.

Mercy: one's will to have compassion for, and, if possible, to alleviate another's misfortune. It is the quality of justice, of making right relations, of knowing our connectedness to all Creation.

I learned these in Grade 8 and decided I would live by them. Acts, not words.

Corporal Works of Mercy:
To feed the hungry.
To give drink to the thirsty.
To clothe the naked.
To shelter the homeless.
To visit the sick.
To ransom the captive.
To bury the dead.

Spiritual Works of Mercy:
To instruct the ignorant – need for knowledge.
To counsel the doubtful – need for certitude, truth.
To confront evil – naming injustice.
To bear wrongs patiently – not seeking revenge.
To forgive offences willingly.
To comfort the afflicted. (And afflict the comfortable?)
To pray for the living and the dead – gratitude and remembrance.

This kind of love requires us to take in the stranger, to open our hearts to the unexpected and welcome it with restraint, no judgments. This kind of love requires imagination and creates possibilities. I think that is the gift in these Acts of Mercy.

Solitude

From a childhood where I should have been protected,
I was robbed of Light. I learned in silence to carve
out my own life. As the eldest, I was programmed for
responsibility and taking care of others. And over the
years I learned to change the theme song of my life script.
I learned that I cannot undo the wrongs of past injustices,
only learn from them. I learned that if you know from
where you came, there is no limit to where you can go.

Apartness
has notes
that touch
the mystic
and the haunted
in me.

Apartness
has sounds
that echo
a lonely song
in the pensive air
of night.

Alone, yet I learn by being in relation to. Every relation
challenges, asks me to respond: the plant needing water,
the e-mail invitation to teach a class, a frozen car, a
news report. I have lived most of my life in groups, yet
ultimately alone. Always feeling the need to respond, to be
available because I have no children of my own. So, I have
given myself away. And been taken. Expanding to the
breaking point and back again. In Light and in Darkness.
To-ing and fro-ing in the quest for balance. Like an atom
dancing in space.

Aloneness became my survival mechanism, the norm. Not feeling. Shutting down. Push – pull. Control – surrender. Abundance – drought. These were/are the polarities of my life in my quest for balance.

Awaken

Enter the dark
but not without a lantern.

When I am not at home in my body I am not at home.
I see. I know. I retreat.
With caution and my wounds.
Can anyone really love Me?

Un enfant souffre en moi	The child within suffers
Depuis longtemps	Hidden for so long
Figé raidi	Frozen stiff
Vivant de douleur	Alive with sorrow
A l'état brut	Raw
Aucun mot	Not a word
Aucun espoir	Not a hope
Aucune caresse	Not a touch
Aucun rayon de soleil	Not a ray of sunshine
Rien	Nothing
Absolument rien	Absolutely nothing
Peut pénétrer	Can penetrate
Ce monde	This world
De solitude	This solitude
Et maintenant	And now
La porte	The door
Est ouverte	Opens
Je peux entrer	I can enter

Over time,
I learned Sacrifice is a response of Gratitude.
That there are countless ways to serve the Universe.
Or say thank you.
I learned Justice is making things whole, bringing
together the broken bits.
I am seeking Beauty.

All works of healing are works of creating Beauty.
I learned that to create is to heal.
I am making my medicine in everyday things like
gardening, kneading bread, writing these reflections.

Water Ways

Water between the rocks breaking through. Swamps, underground springs, artesian wells.

Those are my homeland waters for the first fifteen years of my life. No rivers or lakes in my daily life. The first summer I saw a lake, Moose Lake, it terrified me. My city cousins came for their summer visit and all they wanted was to go to the beach. That was a big trip! Like forty miles! When we went to the bush camp there in springtime, it was before the thaw, it was still frozen. I had no idea how big it was.

Swamps full of swaying medicines. Buttercups and water lilies. Held together by beaver dams. Walking on water underneath me. Going to the well to pull it up clear and cold. Melting snow in winter. Going to the Spring at Butcher Hill on a hot summer day of picking berries. Butcher Hill, the clearing where they dressed the moose or deer before bringing it home.

Bush camps at Whitemouth Lake, Moose Lake, Lake of the Woods. Later I got to know the big Whiteshell Lake and Falcon Lake as places to canoe, camp, renew with friends and family. Some had cottages. I just dropped in. The congregation I joined had an island in Lake of the Woods. For vacation time.

When we moved to the prairies, I encountered the river systems of liquid highways. The La Salle River just by our house was good for skating. A tributary of the Assiniboine (Stone Water people) in Winnipeg Manito'bau – the 'strait of the spirit.' Again, water meeting rock. A drum sound snaking back and forth through the land, joining the Red River at the Forks. Metis ancestors navigating

these waterways, along with Alquonquins down the
St Lawrence and the Great Lakes to get here. Trading.
Forts. Back home.

I guess that is where I get some of my fluidity from.
And some of my rock-solid strength. One of my names is
Nokum Ashini – Grandmother Rock.

Hands

The old woman with heart wide open welcomes me home.
Sit down. Rest.
Night wrapped its arms around me.
I watched her shuffle around the kitchen
looking for the tin of gingersnaps.
She sits in her rocker
one leg out, the other under
picking up her crochet
fingers moving over the thread
like a spider weaving its web
grandma's hands.

How many babies had she guided
into the world
first contact
in those hands?
How many gardens had she planted and hoed
arms getting browner in the summer sun?
Those hands yanking out baby teeth as they loosened
wrapping scarves around resisting necks
kneading dough as if it was a feather
peeling apples in one curled motion
into a pie wedged into perfectly equal triangles
no room to argue over the biggest piece.

Those hands gathering eggs from under hens
without disturbing them.
Wielding an axe cleanly
for kindling.
Circling rosary beads in her lap
lips moving silently
with the rhythm of the words
over and over and over.

That pile of mending and darning
always there.
A torn knee, a hole in a heel, a shirt button gone
all receiving a scolding
as her hand repaired like new again.
The tightness of a newly sewn button
the comforting fresh darn of a sock.
If the damage was too great
scissors would carve out little squares
that later reappeared
transformed on a quilt.

Sitting for hours,
poking her needle in and out of the frame
making little rivers of thread
through all those patches of colours.
She seemed in a trance
her hands circling in and out, over and under
looping the stitches across and back.
Sometimes humming a strange sound
between her teeth
it wasn't a whistle
it wasn't a hum
it seemed to come
from far down inside her
and float out onto the air.

Other times
those hands picked up jars to make
teas and poultices, healing potions and ointments.
Sometimes washing and preparing bodies for burial.
Those hands were messengers
of life and death
rough and ready to do what needed to be done.
Those hands.

Becoming a good ancestor

Now my hands
are the most honest
way I speak
making love
visible
when I have no other way
to reach my heart.

My hands can heal
creating beet chocolate brownies
turning over a blueberry crepe
swirled with whipped cream
as an offering
to feast you
because food
is medicine
and my hands make good medicine.

on a du cœur

grandma said we have heart
on a du cœur

yet sometimes I lose heart

I am warmed and cooled by others
I am nourished by traditions and wisdoms
preserved by many
if I see farther
it is because I am standing on the shoulders of others

I used to be
a ranting raving lunatic
every injustice
every act of corporate greed
everything moved me.
My grandma's quiet constant loving
no questions asked
no questions answered
just simple being
balanced me
together we were
planting seeds, making pies, humming hymns
living from the inside out
on a du cœur

Photo by Marjorie Beaucage.

Religiosity to Spirituality

"my love has made in thee its home;
it cannot be concealed.
My light is manifest to thee;
it cannot be obscured."

—hidden words of Baha'u'llah

Molded out of the clay of love

When I re-member my younger self
I am
immobilized with self-doubt and fear
full of shame and pride
remorse and gratitude
I am
dreaming myself into the me I could be
unravelling the bonds of the past
feeling the now
answering spirit rumblings
vision questing for my purpose in life.

Spiritual quests

"To confirm is to strengthen, to give new assurance of truth, to put past doubt, to sanction."

—Webster dictionary

When I was twelve years old, the Bishop stretched his hands over me, anointed my forehead with oil in the sacrament of Confirmation. Being of vivid imagination, I thought I would be filled with a power going through me like an electric current. I would be instantly transformed with superpowers. Then the slap on the cheek came to remind me that I was going into battle as a "soldier of Christ." I was already a Crusader. Yes, the sacrament was like the spark to ignite the fire within. My feet were shod with the message of shalom, my helmet was wholeness and my sword truth. I would become a soldier for peace in my broken world.

Confirmation was a rite of passage. Deep down in my adolescent soul, I knew I was becoming a woman. Yet even as we, the confirmation candidates, went to the swamp to pick wild yellow buttercups and rose petals to fill our baskets to adorn the bishop's path, I learned that women were not important. He walked on our offerings and paid us no heed.

Still, my younger self prayed regularly. "Most Sacred Heart of Jesus I place my trust in thee." I needed a larger hope. Feeling connected to the seasons. Rogation days. Spring resurrection. Seeds and fields blessed. Rituals and liturgies connecting life mysteries. Acknowledgements of Creation and its many gifts. I felt it all. My grandma sent me to church with the basket of seeds to be blessed, saying "Just in case…" Later, I understood this embracing of both ways with this just-in-case theology.

"The Times They Are A Changin'"

In 1964, right after high school, I joined the Religieuses de Notre Dame des Missions (RNDM). I left home and family. I remember driving to Regina Saskatchewan, the longest trip ever with my parents, everyone crying. My mother was not too keen on me joining the Sisterhood. But I needed something bigger than me. We were poor. University was not an option. And settling down, getting married, having kids was not something I envisioned for myself.

Vatican II was happening, a shifting of the paradigm in the Catholic Church. I was attracted to the edges, theologians thinking outside the box. Teillhard de Chardin appealed to the cosmic dreamer in me. *Le Milieu Divin* connected me to the Earth as a Sacred Place, something I had intuitively felt as a child but had no words for. My portal to wonder was in the natural world. In my religious training I was taught to see the most ordinary aspects of life as contemplation of the divine in everything. Every morning as I donned the holy habit, each item of clothing had a prayer. Every act was a blessing and thanksgiving. An acknowledgement of the Presence of God in all things. Attention to the moment. Being grateful. That was the contemplative life.

Depression, fatigue boredom, irritation, criticism, all was to be lived. What people call depression now, was taught to me as melancholy, a gift to the soul to heal, by going inward and downward to do the heavy work. A constructive force that could be harnessed through prayer and meditation. My prayer journals are full of my pitiful attempts to find myself. Struggling to find my authentic being in each moment. One day I was in the boiler room peeling carrots, feeling down. The novice mistress came in and said: "If you can't peel them with love, don't peel them." Passing another Sister on the stairs. Stopping. Recognizing the presence of God in them. Polishing. Cleaning. All in silence. It is a hard discipline to empty ego self.

In meditation, I was always getting in the way of myself. Doubting and questioning everything. Seeking truth. Asking questions. Moving around. Sharing/living our stories with each other in community. Wanting to express feelings and not knowing how. Where do I put my darkness, my pain, my confusion, my loneliness, my need for closeness? You can have ups without downs, and you can know downs that might not have an up. Live through whatever is in this moment. In this spiritual discipline I learned balance and awareness, striving to manage my intensity.

At one time I thought I had "missed the Sixties" since my experience was so different than many of my contemporaries. No "sex drugs and rock and roll!" But then I remembered a biblical scholar who would come in with the music of Joan Baez, Bob Dylan and Buffy Sainte Marie, saying these were the prophets of our time and that we needed to find new ways to resist the powers of our day. I felt connected to the larger struggles even as I walked the University campus in my habit amid signs saying that "God is dead" and "Chastity is its own punishment." Walking as an alien in this new world, longing to be part of offering possibility. Going to a literature class on Friday afternoon where my American draft-dodger professor rolled out an Indian tapestry carpet, laid out orange wedges and incense and put on a Gregorian chant while he read poetry. I felt strange because in the next moment I was hurrying home to the chapel to actually chant Vespers in Latin. And we can go to the moon and back! I watched the moon landing with awe.

Discovering me

*(I began my religious journey in 1964 as an innocent
novice. I devoted myself completely to the pursuit of
holiness. My idealistic soul thrived. I turned from my
ugly darkness to imagining myself as beautiful.)*

You are a woman.
You are source.
Breeze.
Rose.
Perfume.
Gentleness.
Tenderness.
Whether your facial traits are perfect or imperfect.
You are beauty.
You are and always will be the child with windblown
ringlets bending over a sleeping baby.
The little girl who plaits her sisters' hair and makes
crowns of dandelions.

Even if you walk alone on the road now
you are hand, shoulder, heart open and willing to help.
You are goodness.
You are gift.
You know the secret of joy that comes from nothing.
A pale glimmer, a half-closed curtain, a table adorned
with flowers from your garden.
You know the secrets of love that comes from nothing.
Of that comes from all.

You are and always will be the dike that holds back the
floods of hate.
The bridge thrown between separated relations.

The ark of peace in the torrent of chaos. The refuge.
The haven.
You are the green of April, the rustling leaves, the stump,
strong and tender.
You are weak and fragile, yet it is weakness that is your
very strength.
Glowing flame. Joyous fire.
Light in the darkness of the world. And if you too should
go out...

You are a woman.
You are and you bear in yourself all the women of the
world.
You are and you will be
Eve and Mary until the end of time.

Aware

(From The Small Candle, *a newsletter I started for our community of sisters. Trying to make room for difference. Changing times required dialogue. It was hard for the older ones to adapt to the new order of things that the Church was offering.)*

Aware of myself.
Aware of the world in which I find myself.
Aware of the miseries I left behind.
Aware of others.
Aware of different truths and those who cannot find theirs.
Aware of a troubled world that is searching.
Aware of a world that is perhaps damning itself in its very searching.
Aware of a community.
Aware of the clearsighted, the violent, the searchers, the gifted, and less gifted.
Aware of the humble and less humble, the brave, the timid, the murmuring,
Aware of the needy, and the needed.
All responsible all one.
My Sisters.

Change is hard for some

(*another one from* The Small Candle)

"We have all sensed at the eleventh hour,
a certain quality of human relations.
And in that moment is truth..."

—Antoine de Saint-Exupery

She's old and rigid – the label: conservative. Words keep
stumbling over years and banging into semantic walls.
They do not know how to fit in. The changing rules are
changing their worlds. They are vanishing in emerging
ideas, blowing winds of change chill them to the bone.
They are left standing alone in a crowded solitude.

Before, their lives had security. Their vineyard had limits,
a fixed structure – roles, well learned and lived. And in a
way, love was built – a love without disturbing questions.
Now their world is uneasy...

Good caring women with vision left behind. Young ones
moving ahead – perhaps without direction, perhaps
toward truth. Each one standing alone and lonely. Is there
a way for love to make room?

How shall I name thee

(Theology School, Ottawa 1973)

Deep, deep within the pit of my being
lie the seeds of all that is good and true and beauty-full
an ever-present aching and thirsting
for completeness.

A grasping and losing, and grasping again
something greater than myself
something that breaks through the barriers of my
broken existence
and makes me whole.
I name thee Gift.

Standing in my emptiness
filled with wonder and confusion
letting the gift take root
in the poor soil of my heart.

Roots pushing deep
deeper than I ever dared to go
drawing closer to life's meaning and purpose
hearing a voice.
Come.
I am near. I am here.
Where you are.
Pulsing through your very being.
I name thee Intimacy.

No proof of its source.
No clear vision of whence it comes.
Only an unreachable unfolding presence
covering me, overwhelming me
crying:
Believe. Choose life.
I name thee Distance.

Fire burns
bringing warmth and transformation
beckoning me
to cross over
to enter
to yield to the radically other
to let go of my hold on life
to plunge into the midnight silence
and search out, alone
what I am called to be.
Waiting in the dark
I name thee Light.

Life grows in secret
creating and pro-creating newness
in a strange communion with a presence
within all human experience and more.
Calling me to become
more.

The word is
that I too
am maker
and creator
working to build the earth
the earth needing to be cared for
the stranger needing a friend
the prisoner needing to be set free
the child needing time to grow
the old woman needing hope.

I bring the outside world inside
shape it, connect with it
bring it together
as it was meant to be
in the beginning.
I name thee Creator.

Creating
turns this cockeyed world
inside outside upside down
setting me free
in my wanting and waiting
going beyond
over and over
choosing to live
I name thee Love.

Together we can
make believe
make hope
make love
with the ordinary stuff of our lives
in unexpected and simple ways
when bread is broken and shared
we remember
who we are
singing our song
melodies blending
forming a new harmony
I name thee Mystery.

On the edge again

The edges define the shape that holds me all together.

"I /WE" battle. How can there be a "WE" without strong a "I"?
That inability to recognize differences and honour gifts still
baffles me. Equality is not sameness! My gifts of questioning
are seen as threats.

To know who I am. To know the treasure I carry. The
specialness of my being. And then to recognize this
uniqueness in another. To realize that I am a member of
the human family and so are you. That is what we have in
common. Standing together in wonder at our humanness.
Comfort is the great human gift that creates community.
Enter each other's lives and you will know what you must do.

Work life and community life are poles apart. I want to work
at changing our life together. With respect and a sense of
stewardship for Creation. The institutional church doesn't
give a damn. Time and time again I beat my head against this
patriarchal wall. I rebel against authority. I want out! I am
ready. I am no longer bound by fixed theological structures
that cannot contain the energy of change and imagination.
I am choosing to reshape my life in ways that allow it to flow
and grow into joy, possibility, and wholeness. The charism
of Euphrasie Barbier, the RNDM foundress, is zeal – to be
a contemplative missionary amid the people, in a spirit of
simplicity. I am a zealot!

I need people in the struggle with me. I cannot live in a no
man's land between worlds. Divided against myself. No more
warring or violence to myself. I have endured too much
already. I have taken on the world's injustice; the Church's lies
and my family's wounds. I am choosing to give myself time. I
declare a personal moratorium on all my social involvements.

Breakthrough

"I took a deep breath and listened to the old brag
of my heart. i am i am i am"

—Sylvia Plath

I am becoming fully aware that my life is mine,
what I make it.
Neither church nor state nor man nor job nor anything
can take me from myself
unless I let them.
No more locked-in secrets that create solitudes inside.
"Act justly, love tenderly, walk humbly."

Conformity is a form of death.
Church has always defended authority.
Wanting us to just obey.
The politics of prayer
the political platform of redemption
keeps me and others in a victim place,
waiting to be saved.
"Rescued."

Education for justice
requires a critical awareness
an alternative vision
a spiritual grounding
an understanding of history
hard facts
real knowledge
and practice practice practice.

night

i heard a wail
in my soul
a cry a cry a cry
crying day long out of night
i cannot be comforted
this cannot be
all is not well

what's the matter
the heart-rending cry persists
what is this what is this what is this
this wild space
tamed constrained cannot be
longing so tenderly
to touch the soul

everything else is wind
sowing the wind
reaping the whirlwind
sobbing
i lose
this is the time between
dying and birth
when the truth falls gently
the truth that sets me free

il pleut dans la ville
il pleut dans mon cœur
il pleut partout
écoute tandis que le regret
pleure une ancienne musique
écoute tomber mes liens
je permets la vie
d'entrer

it is raining in the city
it is raining in my heart
it is raining everywhere
i listen while regret
cries an ancient music
listen to my bonds releasing
i am letting life
enter

Finding my way through to the other side

"We are not held back by the love we didn't receive in the past, but by the love we're not extending in the present."

—Marianne Williamson

Balancing my water jar
as if it were the globe itself
jar breaking
releasing
bitter bile eroding my dreams
impossible dreams
holding my biting tongue
my furious gestures
trying to "save my marriage"
time to cast off demons
name them
destroy them
I will not be silent forever
in this wound that love creates
still point of a turning world
touching the ruins of my life.

Leaning hard against a strong wind
falling in a heap when the wind suddenly stops blowing
protecting a hurt
compensating a loss
pushing to overcome an imbalance
patience
it is a walk of hope.

That inner voice again. Others come first. Yet seeking approval, love, validation, and applause from others. Am I giving others the power to define me? Where do I give away my authority when it comes to love, creativity, and pursuing my heart's desires?

That is the work that needs to be done so I can step into more of my power. The old emotional baggage wants to be released, healed, transformed so I can open my heart and feel more loving, happy, and confident.

a time and place to heal

(Homes for Growth at Milner Ridge*)*

> *"...the promise of the holy city is the recognition*
> *that what summons us there was with us*
> *from the beginning: whatever shattering*
> *separations the future may hold..."*
>
> —Apoc. 21:1-6

I am at a threshold in my life. I don't belong in this religious lifestyle. So, what is my mission in life? I travel deep within to where I've never been before, in search of the "sensuous mystic." Allowing myself to feel.

I also seek to understand how my bad experiences in the past have stunted my growth as a sexual being. I am questioning the meaning of my celibacy. Why I chose it in the first place and what there is in it now if anything. How I am "beside myself" having walked around in the valley of darkness for too long.

"Settle in."

I see that I don't need all my defences anymore. Feelings are emerging and causing un-settlings in me. My body is the messenger. Cellular memories are being released as I move energy around through physical work. Physical manual work restores me and makes room inside. Digging roots, making a garden, chopping wood, peeling paint, baking bread, canning tomatoes, clearing whole field of quack grass by hand. And the walls come a-tumbling down. I have loosed my bonds. Trembling I step out in awe before the gift arising from the depth of the earthquake in me and my heart murmurs thank you. Where I was hurt most is where my truth was most denied. I follow the wire of feelings to see where the short circuit is that has been cutting me off from my deepest self.

Meditation on peeling paint off a wall in cabin # 5

(Homes for Growth at Milner Ridge*)*

It is hard to shed the old self to be made new. Flaky layers come off readily. There are nicks and scrapes where there is resistance. One gets crustily comfortable with time. The urge to just cover up the shabbiness with another layer is great. It's a long hard labour to get rid of the old stuff.

Everything here seems to be there for a purpose. The outside and inside jobs all have a meaning for whoever does them. Digging a whole field of quack grass to plant a garden. All is there to draw one closer to the centre of oneself, to the centre of all life. And the question lingers – what about my life? What shall I choose? How will I choose? What is my way to express my gifts? I need to plan my journey. Or maybe not. Maybe I just have to start. Just get up and walk. I have one choice. I am bound to go forward.

Dig. Dig. Dig the field. Lift the weeds. Caress the earth. Uncover. Turn it over. Turn around.

Taking time to clear the garden of my soul and toss away unnecessary garbage so the new can manifest. I feel alive with a powerful awareness of my earth connection. Discern the movements within. And at the end of the day, fireflies flicker the night away.

There is a part of me that I uncovered. The part that commissions me to break new ground. To till it and prepare it for planting. Then move on when others move in to settle it. I am called to pick up my axe and hack away at another bit of brush and clear the path. That seems to be my mission in life. Helpers mirroring me to myself. Feeling loved and affirmed by friends.

Letter of encouragement from Sister Claire: I really believe in you and that you will have the courage to live what you must live. I believe also, for you leaving the community is not leaving but moving from one stage in fidelity to another stage. You are being faithful to yourself and to who you are in growth. You are precious to me and will always be. I am not sad as I see you take the direction you are taking because I know that that is the only way you will become all that you can become. I am only happy that I am sharing in this ever expanding you. Believe in my very deep love for you. I carry you in my heart.

I never learned 'culture'

Just lived it. No talk about it. Hiding in plain sight.

The earth... the air... the fire... the water... return return return return.

My spirit returned to the elements. I turned to the cultural camps and ceremonial revivals that were happening across the Land once it was no longer a criminal offense to do ceremony. Because of the colonial legacy of the churches, it didn't take long for me to see the patriarchy alive and well in the Lodges as well. Women's medicine and Two Spirit gifts and place were not respected. Men were laying down the rules for how we were supposed to be as women. I had done my time with rules!

I remember going to Morley Cultural Camp in the summers. All male led. To the Midewiwin Lodge at Roseau River. Movements that didn't have room for youth, women and children, grandmothers, Two Spirit or artists. Isn't everyone equal in the Circle?

My teacher Art Solomon said, "Women are the Medicine," and I asked him what he meant when he said we should be picking up our medicines. We had many heated conversations about the role of women. If women are so sacred, then why don't they build us Moon Lodges instead of shaming us when we are on our time? He was one of the few feminist Elders I knew. He always had my back.

Grandmother Spider

Courage my sister
Letting your dark shine bright
Uncovering stones of history

I remember First Woman
Grandmother Spider
She birthed herself from the dark void
It took a long long time
For She had nothing to work with
Except the power of her own thought
She dreamed her thought into substance
And as soon as She was born
She began to spin and spin and spin
She wove that Sacred Spiral
Upon which the Universe was born
And that is the thread I cling to now

Recipe for a good day

Waniska! Get up!
Make your bed
Give thanks for a new day
Wash your face
Give thanks for the water
Smudge
Give thanks for your life
Prepare food
Give thanks for nourishment
Set your intention
Be present
Moment to moment
Stay open to surprises
Give thanks for the gifts you receive
Give thanks
Give thanks
Give thanks

Photo by Marjorie Beaucage.

I am a Woman

*I took a deep breath and listened to the
old brag of my heart. i am i am i am*

—Sylvia Plath

Le féminisme c'est quoi?

C'est une façon de voir,
                    It is a way of seeing,
de percevoir le monde.
                    of perceiving the world.

Percer au travers des murs
                    Piercing through walls,
des obstacles
                    obstacles,
de tout ce qu'on nomme 'oppression'.
                    everything we name 'oppression'.
C'est une façon d'agir,
                    It is a way of acting,
de faire des liens entre tout,
                    of making links, connecting the dots,
de changer les relations de pouvoir
                    of changing power relations
dans ce système patriarcal
                    in this patriarchal system we are in.

C'est un mouvement de femmes de cœur
                    It is a movement of soul sisters
qui questionnent les règles du jeu de domination.
                    who question the rules of the game.

C'est moi, c'est toi, c'est toute la collectivité
                    It is you. It is me. All of us collectively
reconnaissant notre pouvoir au féminin.
                    recognizing our woman power.

To be a woman

To be a woman is to know that change implies break-up of the world as one has known it... the loss of the known makes room for the new. Tuning in to my moon cycle with its ebb and flow, to find the rhythm of my life. Process is nature.

To be a woman is to be subversive. Political visions and dreams for a different world are meshed with spiritual continuity. We have roots. We are home. In our bodies we open deeper and deeper, and wider and wider. We reverberate life in the spaces and distances between, echoing out of ourselves into a wider world. Women have always known about survival and interconnectedness. The separation of self from spirit is an imposed dichotomy that goes against being. When we no longer acknowledge our connectedness to everything we get out of balance.

My compassion runs deep. I am free. I will not drown in old pain. The river flows and there are good trees on the banks to rest and heal there.

I am aware I am not meant to be alone. I don't have to change the world. I am a visionary. I have gifts to challenge and call forth others. I am radical. I am woman.

I walked through the tunnel of my life and the veil was lifted. And doors opened quietly and peacefully. Two things: needing to find my identity in terms of belongingness and sexuality.

A sense of mystery that new life is possible. I am
filled with joy beyond words. I am free. Overflowing.
Running over. Oozing with the juice of life. Penetrating.
Permeating every pore.
I am home.

The container of me is changing. I know that I am
a spiritual sensuous mystic and need to express my
creativity in honest ways. And in relation. I know my
spirit needs nurturing and I will see to that. I know that
the numb spot in my sexuality will be revived in time
through the evacuation of memories and the welcoming
of newness. Turning and turning we come around right.
Respect and awe and gratitude for support and love and
friendship.

Mystic Recipe

Give up "to have" in order to attain freedom "to be."

Ingredients for becoming a mystic:
        Strongly romantic temperament
        innate simplicity and ardor
        total self-giving
        "all-or-none" attitude
        extreme sensitiveness
        great power of endurance
        strong will
        peculiar makeup of genius
        courage and generosity
        gaiety and awe
        close kinship with the earth
        fighter and dreamer fused into one

Wounded Healer

Je ne suis plus le guerrier blessé
je suis la guerrière guérie.

Je change mes vœux de pauvreté, de chasteté,
et d'obéissance
en vœux d'abondance, d'amour et de respect.

Quand une personne part pour la Terre Promise,
il faut renoncer au pays des ténèbres.

Au-delà des frontières ce sont des vieilles affaires,
des vieux vêtements.
On ne peut à la fois rester et partir.

On part vers la lumière.

I am no longer the wounded warrior
I am the healed warrior.

I am changing my vows of poverty, chastity and
obedience
to vows of abundance, loving and respect.

When someone sets out for the Promised Land,
they must leave behind the dark.

Beyond the boundaries are only old things, old garments.
One cannot stay and go.

Go toward light.

Small 's' sister

At a conference. Listening to Angela Miles. Becoming
aware of my radical vision of my womanhood and
celibacy. It is not a narrow politic but a personal
transformation and awareness of my power to love.
I desire to remember who I am, before trying to be who
I am not.

Agents of Social Change: a six-day Christian feminist
conference at Cedar Glen, Boulton Ontario, Canada.
A theological reflection on our experience as women.
Feeling my aloneness. My woundedness. My wanting.
Small 's' sisterhood confirmed. Yes. I have to leave RNDM
Sisters. I cannot go back. I can only go forward. I am
home. In me. I am standing on sacred ground. There is
more room in my house.

The Women's Movement defined by feminist academic
theory is often a very closed system; classist and mostly
racist, because it does not recognize cultural difference.
I've always had a hard time with this lack of awareness.
Cultural values are different in a Black community,
Indigenous community, Chinese community. I learned
this in the Philippines when I saw the people struggle
for their liberation against the Marcos regime. I saw the
role women played in that struggle and how the Women's
Movement tried to influence. Gabriela, the women's sector
in the Philippines, took stands. When children are hungry
and there is no clean running water, you know you're
fighting for health, because you're dying of diarrhea.
The Women's Movement here does not take on issues
like hunger and the need to keep a family together. I do
not think they respect family and different structures of
decision making. There is no such thing as a single-issue
struggle because we do not live single issue lives.

Women's conferences are still the most patriarchal events. They don't know what a Circle is and what real equality is. We could teach them so much – and I've tried. Every single conference I have been to, it's the same thing. They haven't learned anything. They still have panels and one-way communication, and this guest star thing. If it's truly a Women's Movement, they should have learned by now that's not how women talk to each other. I've complained about these matters all along the way, and I've hung in there. I was unofficially part of the Canadian delegation of the Canadian National Action Committee (NAC) in Beijing. Some friends have recognized the same challenges, but change is slow because the politics, strategies and protocols are still patriarchal. The Movement has not yet created truly feminist forms.

As a movement it does not appeal to me. It is not where I feel comfortable and myself. There is no room for me there. I don't like to debate, because that's a win-lose situation, not an exploration. Indigenous women? Invisible. A lot of us individually have tried at various times to participate. Still, they have never come to participate in our Circles, our gatherings, or events. It is always one-way. We go to their events on their platforms, but they do not come to ours. Say if the National Action Committee President came to town, why would we all have to go to her meeting? Why couldn't she come and sit in our Circle?

That's always the case for us. We're always in a strange land.

New York Lower East Side Catholic Worker

Pilgrimages have been a way to expand my world. Immersing myself into the unknown, seeking to find the festival side of life amid the woundedness is my path to uncovering who I am in relation. I heard a passage of the *Long Loneliness* read when I was just eighteen. It is about Dorothy Day, anarchist, war resister, justice seeker. "Workers of the world unite. All you have to lose is your chains." Words that vibrated my being. Karl Marx spoke them earlier. What a gift. This call to free my bonds. The Catholic Worker is a movement. A way of life based on the works of mercy. Dorothy Day and I are kindred spirits. I went to New York in 1976 to live and work in a House of Hospitality for the summer. And I was honoured to live alongside her in her humble truthful way.

Reaching out with beggar hands for bread
the more I sought the less I had.

Daily sorrows
tired hearts
broken dreams
betrayals
bread salted with tears of hope
our common human ground.

Loving with all my soul and all my heart and all my mind knowing an inner freedom great enough to embrace all that exists.

Being present.
Waiting.

Women are teachers

Educare: To nurture. To care.

I was trained to be a teacher at Brandon University; that is the work I am expected to do as a Sister. After less than three years in the classroom, I cannot continue to impose this way of learning on children.

I know I am not in the right place as far as teaching in the school system goes. I do not do well in power structures that are hierarchical and patriarchal. Choosing to teach according to my values I re-arrange my classroom, reform curriculum, make relations with parents. I cannot follow the system's rules.

In the liberation movements of popular education in South America, I discover Paulo Freire and Augusto Boal empowering people through literacy. I learn to read our lived experience, acknowledge and tell our own stories, and together we begin to clearly see the need for change. Moving away from oppression to having power to transform is a powerful lesson.

I am no longer bound by fixed structures that cannot contain the energy of change and imagination. I am choosing to reshape my life in ways that allow it to flow and grow into joy, possibility, and whole-ness.

Recipe for change

At the Popular Theatre Alliance of Manitoba (PTAM),
we were able to create a wondrous event, *The Learners
Connection: Taking Action – a Manitoba Literacy
Conference.* We passed on skills and awakened creativity
for participants of literacy classes across Manitoba, urban
rural and northern. This also included writing literacy
policies for the government.

Mix together:
        9 creative women
        1 large cup of life
        1 lb. of hard work and determination
        1 spoon full of courage
        1 pinch of good humor
        1 sprinkling of wit

Blend with a generous helping of community friends and
family

Yield: A new play from the *Journeys* literacy group and
their story: *Under the Line* – a witty down-to-earth look at
life on welfare. Produced by the *No Name Brand Welfare
Clan Theatre.*

Turning to Mary Kay

"Whatever you vividly imagine, ardently desire, sincerely believe and enthusiastically act upon must inevitably come to pass."

—Mary Kay Ash

Mary Kay is one of my teachers. She started a movement creating an independent business model for women to take charge of their own lives. As a woman, I needed to soften some hard edges. I am broke and broken. Another re-build. So for two years, in the late 1990s, my time as a Mary Kay consultant paid my mortgage, and I learned to accept praise and encouragement.

The most important tool for success is the belief that you can succeed. Attitude. Belief. Commitment. The ABCs of Mary Kay values: Integrity and fairness, service, enthusiasm, praise, teamwork, leadership, priorities, balance. A down-to-earth approach to making dreams come true. A way based on women's values of cooperation and support.

At first, I could hardly stand all the positivity and praise. "Those who achieve success, are those who take a dream and make it come true," says Mary Kay

Reaching beyond self-imposed limitations, I could find new dreams to follow. A catalyst to choose to do something different. Explore positive being. Hang up my hang-ups. Be good to myself. Feel good about the effort. Accept praise.

It is all a choice. I want a stable income. I want to be rewarded and affirmed for what I do. I can make my dreams come true. I can reward myself based on my efforts. Choose people that are positive to be with. Self-sabotage is in my head! 1300 words per minute in my subconscious mind. Painful assumptions and perceptions set by age six! To re-form our imagery and self-talk towards a healthy sense of self with nurture and praise instead of a foundation of judgment and fear. What an awesome lesson.

I'm undoing my feminist conditioned response to makeup. I remember when I was growing up, my mother had one tube of lipstick. She only wore it on special occasions like the Saturday night dances. I watched her change from feeling ordinary to feeling beautiful as she put it on. Transformation comes in many ways.

On turning 30

For once in my life
I experience the deep sense of joy at being born.

I witness my own unfolding and growing into the me that
I am.
What a gift
to stand on the threshold of possibility
alive to my vision.

I lay bare the wounds for healing
I see how much is lost if I deny
the fruit of my own experience.

Altogether is a beautiful moment

My new relationship is life giving. Opening me up.
Bearing the beams of love. Choosing to grow together.
Plumbing my depths with someone who is not afraid
of me. Clarity. Challenge. Support. Affirmation. In my
search for me. When I tell my story, it helps me to get in
touch with my feelings and to name what has happened
to me. Even the cold-blooded hate towards my father for
robbing me of my woman self. Earthquakes of pain erupt.
Remembering desecration. My greatest pain. Where my
sacredness is buried.

First kiss

A world flew into my mouth
with our first kiss
and its wings were dipped
in all the flavours of grief.

O my darling
tell me what love can mean in such a world.
You touched
with so much gentleness
my darkness.
You brought me clarity.
Gift after gift I wear.

If I have known beauty
let's say I came to it asking.
To sit emptily
in the sun
receiving fire
that is the way to mend.
Sitting perfectly still
and only remotely human.
Did you ever see a closeup of rain falling on the water?
Droplets of rain fall
Change into spinning tops
as they touch the surface
spiral together
in a dancing circle.
Laughing and giggling all the while.

Sky is dancing
with meteors and flashes of lightning
catching the beating of my heart.

The wind
the night
the trees
caress and comfort me.
Fire warming.
Woodsmoke rising.

Loving my woman self
woman to woman.
Coming to my senses
with artichokes and songs.
Birkenstocks, plaid shirts and overalls
making visible this new sisterhood.

Ebb and flow

*Go deep enough and there is a bedrock of truth,
however hard.*

—May Sarton

You, May Sarton, always have the soul words I need to
embrace myself in my solitude. I stand knee-deep in the
flow of life and pay close attention. I have been led to the
right paths, friends, meaningful work. I have been blessed
many times when I trust this flow, depending on the
Universe to take care of me. This flow of Grace moving
me, moving me to the right livelihood, companions,
destiny. Freed from fears of abandonment, demands,
expectations as I become gentler and more compassionate
with myself.

Everything is stripped away. Again. I am mourning the
self I abandoned. Again. Greeting this self like one might
greet a lover at the end of a long and costly war. Again.
Compassion for the emptiness. Again.

Valentine's day

words seem inadequate
but words are all I have
as I wrestle my spirit
searching for my song of life
did you ever feel
half as lonely as I
who
wishing to feel
and wanting to stay
stayed
until my hypocrisy rose choking
and I went out into that cold night
where nothing was there to feel
except a sometime imagined
coldness
which was not as comfortless
as my damned numbed soul
sucked into that dark and lonely hole
i will not bear this loneliness

i journey back
to all those endings and beginnings
inside me
all those uncertain doubting times
coming all the way
inside me
then
all of me
coming back into
life
born from this loneliness of loving
and the wisdom of my senses
choosing this truth

For my child

it has been many days
and many of the longest nights
that the forgotten child
has stood pressed against
the library window of my dream
somewhere
between asleep and waking
it has come forth
to find me

from pages
of stories unheard
never fully gone
never fully here

lost child stands
pressed against the inner wall
of my own flesh
never fully turned away
never fully loved

Love is powerful

"to love means to establish ties"

—Antoine de St-Exupéry, *The Little Prince*

The gift I am uncovering: How to use my loving power, express my sexuality. I want to be intimate with people. With women. I am eager for love. I want my heart to be in harmony with my life.

I desire to remember who I am.

What lives in me naturally is compassion, gentleness, creativity, joie de vivre, gratitude for all the wild and wonderful. When I experience goodness in my life, I feel a harmony deep down. I feel blessed and gifted. It fills up my senses. C'est si bon!

Sweet sweet loving

I dream I am precious rock touching the
edge of you that needs the moon's loving.

—Audre Lorde

Reclaim. Rehome. Restore.

My dreams, the imbalances, the myths, the strength of
women – all beautiful to me today. Sitting firmly inside
love, I feel joy. Luxuriate. Waking to the feel and scent of
love lingering. Feeling happy and warm inside. Embracing
the whole world. Love expands. Ravish me again and
again. I am inside of love. I am altogether. Whole. I have
been waiting all my life for union such as this. I love the
rapture of being undone and the depths it spins me to.

Endings and beginnings...

*The experience of union goes hand in hand
with that of separation...to find also means to lose.*

−Aldo Carotenuto, *Eros and Pathos:
The Shades of Love and Suffering*

Breaking up is hard to do.

There are no models to mend the broken-hearted.
Sorting out my lost wholeness and sense of abandonment.
Losing the erotic element of a relationship.
Great courage is needed to face the ruin that has been
wrought in one's soul.
To believe love is not lost even if the loved one is.
Slowly mist rises.
A new morning awaits me.

Blue moon

I can't bear to sweep out all of you
love is before you
yet it is after you
never the same again.

You have decided my fate,
breaking cold turkey.

Wherever you are
be fearless
grow by your strength
of your fighting
for your self
your life
apart from me
but vivid
as when we were one.

There is no way to love without being changed

You chose another.

Space lengthening between us
And I, all tangled impulses and yearnings
the little seed of the pursuit of joy turning to anguish.

We did this
let ourselves downward
hand over hand as on a rope.
We did this
conceived of each other
conceived each other in a darkness
which I remember as drenched in light.

Kind of my kind
earth of my earth
wave of my wave
want of my want
your touch outlining the edge of my dance.

Now, I look out the window
and stare at the blue clothesline
lined with raindrops
soft faith gone
up in the air.
I am hoping to land on my feet
living ever separate
ever connected.

Our souls have touched
regardless of gender
regardless of form
regardless
so having undone me
will you
gather me kindly
and show me
how the goddess dances
balancing the world as she spins
through all the weathers
weaving ribbons for the moon
with her tears.

Love lessons

I remember the winter I spent cutting wood
yelling and screaming my insides out
all the while
moving energy around

Come spring I had some woodpile
fire for the revolution
resentments fears betrayals dead dreams
gone to ash now
truth is in bits and pieces
not all at once

Lessons from "The Book of Tactics" for a Princessa

Think through the body. Feel it. The chronic negativity lying dormant.
Always and Never is weary and despairing. Move it out. It is disabling the power to act.
Abandon revenge. Refuse to harm others.
Behave as if the enemy is your ally. And accept changes.
Build a network of support. Accept no outside support, only insiders. Keep focused. No strings attached to support.

Become like the enemy. Create ambiguity. Ask 'what happened?'
Bare essentials. See it for what it really is. Reveal simple clear truths.
Oppose power. Do not fight it directly. Dis-believe in prevailing power. No drama left.
Behave as if you've already won this battle and create the new.
Study every situation for its opposite. Play out contradictions.
Be ready to get hurt and yet not inflict hurt.
Be true when everyone is hidden.
Be open when everyone is armored.

Invite any suffering, even loss or humiliation, rather than show that your ego is more important than the shared goal. Envelop and contain flaws.
Introduce something new to destroy a boundary: Curiosity. Affection. Shrewd understanding. Laughter.
Cultivate the young. Enlarge your circle. Open your mind.
Surprise. Stand tall. Say what you want. Declare it. Act it.

Slow things down. Hold your breath. Breathe. Wait. Do not rush into action. Pausing gives the advantage of rest and preparation.

Appeal to the 'better self.' Fill the spirit with poetry, story, possibility, song. Crumble the foundations of self-sabotage.

The last power is the power of goodbye. If you've tried everything to unbuild, tear down, end the battle, and the opponent remains an adversary, walk away. Withdraw. Save your spiritual initiative for another day. Know what to end and when to end it. Destroy the dead things in life, like a forest fire prepares barren ground for new growth. Being strong about saying *No* means that every *Yes* is real.

Enter.

Excerpt from conversations with sky woman

Is a leader always first? Do you have to have followers?
What is a role model anyway?

Role: play out ideas, vision, e-motions, act out, act on.
Model: to shape, to fashion, to change.

What is our power?

Grandmother Moon is the source
teaching us to govern
the power of seeing the heart's details
the power of knowing what makes people hum and whirl
the power of listening to the unsaid
the power of probing silences for meaning
the power of saying the truth
the power of being open when everyone else is armored
the power of enlarging space
the power of respecting difference
the power of eroding hidden boundaries.

(And by the way, boundaries do not really keep things
out... they lock you in.)

Honour your sacred self.
Celebrate the joy freedom fearlessness
of being a daughter of Sky Woman.

Collage by Marjorie Beaucage. Photo by Barbara Reimer.

you gotta walk it like you talk it

The radical is that unique person who actually believes what they say. Liberals protest, radicals rebel. Liberals become indignant. Radicals become fighting mad and go into action. Liberals do not modify their personal lives. Radicals give themselves to the cause.

—Saul Alinsky, Reveille for Radicals, 1975

Intention is everything

I am using my creativity, designing educational approaches for systemic change at the grassroots level. My simple yet challenging approach is first, to set the intention. That is the core of the work. What is needed? What cultural value system am I in? What are the ways of being and relating in this community? Language is a way of thinking and being in the world, a way of organizing life. There is more than one way to say or do something. No judgments. Cultural biases. Ask questions. Break it down. Identify the parts to work with/on. Ask what they know. Build on it. Talk from Self. Make mistakes. Analyze what happened, overcome the obstacles. Reinforce what worked. Celebrate learnings. Give encouragement and do ongoing evaluation to adjust course of action going forward. Decide what comes next. Create alternatives. Choose together. Adapt skillfully and be clear in purpose. As for timing, it is everything. As Leroy Littlebear said: "Culture is a collective agreement."

Philosophy of Social Change

*"I see you now, with all your puzzling aloofness
disassociating yourself from players and games
because you've already figured out who the winners
and losers are going to be and you refuse to ignore
your own conclusions"*

—Leon Uris, *Trinity*

In the time when I thought I knew everything, in
my arrogance and unknowing wisdom of my early
thirties, I had this theory of oppression/domination.
Domination is any situation where a group of people are
crushed by institutional powers, to force them to accept
living and working conditions that benefit those that
dominate. Since the industrial era (and rise of capitalism)
knowledge, technologies, systems have constituted
privileged tools of domination over other peoples, classes,
nations, creating power imbalances and injustices.
Corporate power/bureaucracy is basically self-serving
and protects itself. Political and social structures as we
understand them are things of the past, and the crisis
through which we are now passing is nothing but the full
and inescapable manifestation of their falsity.

I always thought that the worst invention of the Industrial
Age was the clock. It made time into money, and it has
been that way since. Or is it the alphabet that freezes
stories in time as the only truths. What is not written does
not have the same validity somehow. And knowing how
to read allows information to come into your mind in
very selective predetermined ways.

Structures of domination: Schools – students without power and voice. Structuring learning based on the power of knowledge holders. The school system is a legal institution where children must be 'sent' to learn how to serve the product-oriented capitalist agenda instead of nurturing human aspirations and dreams. They are inculcated with a content-based knowledge that indoctrinates while deculturing any other knowledge forms they may have lived in before coming to school. The rules of obligations, prohibitions and discipline are imposed from above without consultation, leading to dependence or revolt. Universities reinforce the existing systems and train the elites to take their place within that system.

How shall you free yourself from it... if you are underdog or middledog or topdog?

Churches too are pyramidical structures aligned with the state. Evangelization and colonization intertwined for 'civilizing,' acculturating, de-structuring and devaluing – outlawing existing traditional self-governing relational systems and replacing them with systems that create dependency and competition (divide and conquer). The establishment of laws and norms destined to limit freedom adopted by a 'silent and submissive majority' to marginalize, attack or suppress those who seek other ways of life. Silence. Forbid. Isolate. Count on collusion.

For twenty centuries we have seen many Christians not even beginning to understand or live the Gospels. Why do we lack the courage to do so and waste so much energy and cause so much pain over non-essentials? Woman power wasted. Lord have mercy. So many contradictions.

When innovation goes too far or comes too close

Sometimes we need to risk failure
to learn
to face the uncomfortable ambiguities of a new context
to see our assumptions about how events should be
organized
since they are so internalized
they are perceived as norm-al.
Questioning how we view the world is dangerous and
threatening
even as we desire change.

Naming.
Developing a critical consciousness
to shape the future
is an open process.
There is no final word on it.
It means recognizing incoherence, contradictions
putting our judgments on the table.
It means to reflect, to refuse, to choose, to go beyond
that is what leads to creation.

One-day workshops with groups who are not groups
are not effective in promoting change.
Being truly responsible for oneself
and one's learning seems too revolutionary a concept.
De-schooling professionals is a challenge.
A lifelong task!

The minimum is the ability to question.
The maximum would be the ability to woo new
combinations
a not-yet kind of dreaming and visioning
providing more time for incubation and nurturing new
insights
shaped out of a tension between the current situations
we find ourselves in
and the vision we have.

The future continues to break in upon us
as we shape and reshape our practice.
The future is already here.

We have tested each other's waters, now we must drink
from our own well.

Peace Movement

*All the arms in the world don't offer
the security of one embrace.*

—New Internationalist Magazine

Warring and peacemaking.
How will we break the power of structures that set people
against each other as enemies?
How do we give up the desire for power over others?
The whole system that uses power and violence to oppress
others is numb.

Resistance.
Not the "Battle Hymn of the Republic" that makes us
righteous ones.
Good guys and bad guys scenario.
Us and them.
No such thing as holy wars or just wars.
Pure madness.

Peace can be established through justice making.
Prevent the face of 'other' from being demonized.
Refuse to deal with each other as enemies.
Let the sorrow in.
Express the fears.
Make room to breathe.
To act.

Tears break down barriers when no other form remains.
Weeping allows newness.
Solidarity.
Cleansed and renewed.

When you are despairing, you cannot see how a future can exist out of such a horrible now. Someone must face the darkness and be trusted to hold it.
To contradict it.
To uncover our deep concerns and caring for the world
To get to know each other from that hurting place.

What do you love about this Earth? What causes you pain for the world?
What gifts, stories, talents do you bring? What do you need?
What ground are you standing on?
What will keep you going when the going gets tough?
Can you imagine the world you want to be in?

If we can dream it, we can do it.

Activist self-care recipe

Collect ingredients for creating rituals: candles, medicines, stones
Make an altar space
Prepare food offerings
Gather a community of friends
Nurture and support each other
Share stories of struggles and joys
Remember who we are together in ceremony
Turn the compassion we have for the world towards ourselves.

Repeat as needed.

UN youth seminar

The major activity of the prophet was interference.
—Rabbi Heschel

What power do youth have?

Much of my work through the years has been with youth, equipping them with tools for change. The power to challenge assumptions and values, fixed positions is what they bring me. And I asking youth to consider – what is a paradigm shift? What would happen if as a peacemaking action, you organized a campaign for all the students in your school to boycott all competitive sports that create win/lose situations and offered an alternative way to play and develop physical discipline and team skills.

When I asked a group of youth to consider this, there was such immense sadness… they could not see it. So much to unlearn.

So I tell them:
Circle what you love.
Again, and again.
You are a blessing.
Claim your ground.
Befriend the dark –
the dark has its own light.
Risk courage.

Philippines ATORS

(Actor Teacher Organizer Researcher)

> *Beyond the darkness, the griefs, the iron bars*
> *and barbed wire, the pain is our birthright*
> *and the hope of food and freedom for all in the*
> *tomorrows that will come.*
>
> – Karl Gaspar

In 1985, I went to the Philippines on an 'Exposure Tour'
organized for Canadian activists, unionists and church
leaders seeking to learn from the human rights struggles
and be in solidarity. It was my first trip outside of Canada.
I experienced 'culture shock' amidst the struggle for
democracy and human rights. Karl Gaspar is the first
person we met, just released from prison after being
detained for almost two years. I had written to him
in prison. His eyes tell the tale he cannot tell. Wells of
sadness.

'Situationers': A way to look at a situation together and
develop our own theories from practice. What I conclude:
The needs of the poor take priority over the wants of
the rich. The freedom of the dominated takes priority
over the liberty of the powerful. The participation of the
marginalized takes priority over the preservation of an
order that excludes.

Visiting a 'free trade zone' workers' labour school at
Bataan, it felt more like a high school, the workers in
training seem so young. Taken away from families in the
country and brought here to work in horrid conditions.
Still, their eyes glowing like stars beneath thatched roofs,
they are organizing, despite repressive government

decrees. Making Barbie dolls, Nike runners, and Ford vehicles. Some young women are promised work and then taken to the Clark Airforce Base and Subic Naval Base- American bases from which the United States fought the Vietnam War. Now a carnival of flesh; please hear what we dare not say... please do not forget us.

I join cultural workers travelling, community to community, explaining issues using masks and theatre on church steps. They are raising morale by placing the means of art in the hands of the people. People to people. Issue to issue. Local campaigns.

I am overwhelmed time and time again. 2560 workers employed at DOLE. 40,000 cartons of pineapple a day! 10,800 cans an hour x 20 lines – mostly women, getting rheumatism from the juice. Tight security watching every move. If workers have an accident, they are suspended, so many accidents go unreported. American music blaring above the noise of machines – a cultural invasion.

So, what is "good news"
to a worker in a factory who only eats once a day and earns only 13 pesos
to a farmer planting onions for the USA and whose costs of production places him in debt
to a fisherman in a subdivision lake controlled by big foreign trawlers
to a tribal chief driven from ancestral lands by multinationals
to a young woman 'hospitality girl' for American servicemen and tourists
to a mother whose sons have been salvaged by the military
to a child whose parents have disappeared.
What is "good news?"

On a stop to photograph bananas being picked on a plantation, we are held up by security for taking pictures of the operation. They take our film. Del Monte protects its methods. This delay means we are on the road after dark. The hour when the fanatics are out strafing villages, keeping the people in fear. Four goons appear out of the ditch and stand on the road. Our jeepney driver lunges around them as they fire at us as we hunker down on the floor.

A meeting of tribal people is scheduled in the North Lauzon province: the parliament of the hills. Four hours on the local rural bus. I sit beside a woman who has six children tumbling from her lap into the aisle, and a man with a live rooster on his knee. There is an American tourist with a 'hospitality girl.' A gun pointed at me rests on the lap of the soldier across from me. We arrive in the middle of a field. Some of the chiefs are late, the river was too high for crossing. I couldn't help noticing their bare feet – so ancient, so huge, melding with the earth. They tell stories, share their problems and come to some common understanding of what is happening to them and why. My land is being stolen by Christians. No one will die of hunger if we unite. We are victims of fear of the military. Fire above, fire below – caught between two fires. That dam will ruin us. We have to move again. The meeting continues for days. Somehow everyone had a mat to sleep on, a bowl of rice and salt fish to eat. In the midst of it all, decisions are made to unite and stand together.

Going south. We meet fishermen relocated on a mountain for port expansion in the name of free trade. Now there is no access to the sea to feed their families. Farmers without land. Eyes are on us. No place to go. Villages demolished. More people relocated. Bulldozers are waiting for the foreigners (us) to leave to do their dirty deed.

May 1st is not a party!

On International Workers Day, morning begins with briefings and preparations for the march. Wet towel for tear gas, running shoes to run, hat for the sun (it is 33° C), extra shirt in case of water bombs and delays. High noon, blazing sun, foreigners (our cohort) lead the delegation – less chance of violence they say. Orderly ranks, eight columns converging from all directions. 800,000 people in the streets despite Marco's warning. Arrived in Bonifacio Square and we are surrounded by military. Clapping, slogans, songs, poetry, speeches all night long. We cannot leave. Oceans of tears and rivers of blood bind people together as they take their history and move towards their dreams of a Philippines for Filipinos, recognizing that individual courage becomes collective strength.

C.U.T. goes to Newfoundland 1978

Newfoundlanders are tired of serving as a 'charitable organization' for other provinces in Canada, foreign corporations and companies.

–Now that we've burned our boats

One of the most influential social movements of my life was the Canadian Urban Training (C.U.T.) for social action and justice, begun in 1965. Social analysis and action were grounded in an examination of values, assumptions, hopes and fears – an action-reflection model. The training was created to go beyond the 'charity' model of helping, and teaching church and community leaders to look at social action through a justice lens. Part of the tradition was to get together for training and reflection. The trip to Newfoundland was a most memorable one for me. And my connections to the Rock are strong still.

When a great wave breaks on the rocky incline of shore, all that marshalled strength shatters into countless foamy fragments. The wave has lost its familiar undulating strength, returning to the sea, which is itself. The watcher knows with certainty only that another wave will come. And it will be a new experience. The process is eternal – wave will follow wave – but there will be a difference. No wave is exactly like another.

Like life. We may think of the moment the wave breaks as becoming a moment of self-discovery when everything breaks open. The act has been spent. A moment of reflection. The bonds of purpose are loosened. And the questions are heard again. Who am I? What is my purpose? For we are human beings in search of meaning. Whether the wave is a rising undulation or a breaking roar of defiance on the rocks, a thousand spattered blots merging with the sea, it is a sound which persists and sweeps us above the tumult of time into a new way of being human together. For there is a sense that the Great Mother makes everyone feel important, everyone is sacred. And newness is born.

To be is better than not to be!
That is the answer

(apologies to Shakespeare)

Delicatesse supreme
blueberry clusters hugging hillsides
barren dorm-style bunkhouse
warmed by sharing
territorial rights
giving way to self help

Cool deep waterfall pools
sun-kissed yoga on the shore
fireside's fish and brews
early morning sunrise on Signal Hill
leave-takings and passovers are part of it
women at the heart of it
please continue…

Solidarity comes in various forms shapes and sizes

It is not good for people to wait all the time.
Although I remember still the beating of drums.
The chanting that has no metaphor. Slow death in
Whitedog brings no more tears to my eyes.
Tragedy on a winter cold reserve is so common a
relative of people that I cannot cry anymore.

—G. Kenny Whitedog's Cat Dance Community Theatre

My first protest: Reed's Greed, at the Winnipeg Art Gallery in the early 1970s. Nervously handing out leaflets to people in fur coats going in for the art opening. Asking them to boycott this exhibition sponsored by corporate greed. The Reed Paper company dumping mercury laced waste into the English-Wabigoon River system resulting in Minamata disease for Indigenous people eating the contaminated fish.

Later, the struggle to protect Dene Lands and Rivers: protesting the Mackenzie Valley Pipeline.

Project North and the boy-boys: constantly facing the arrogance of national offices and governments deciding the agenda and strategies without local consultation. NOTHING ABOUT US WITHOUT US. This was my ongoing struggle with patriarchy. Daily facing the Man! Power Over. Top Down. Standing with Indigenous nationhood dreams of Dene people at the Berger Inquiry into the Mackenzie Valley Pipeline. The song of the people, the land of the people... the will of the people must win.

Anishinaabe Park Occupation: My suggestion to other church people: "Afraid to be on the line? Well you can make sandwiches and bring blankets." Solidarity is practical like food and warmth.

Griffin Steel Strike

*"I'm mad as hell and
I'm not going to take it anymore"*

−fundraiser button I made with quote
borrowed from *Network* movie.

The strike is about Chilean refugees willing to risk it all,
striking against compulsory overtime. For the forty days
of Lent, I went to lay my body down against this injustice.
A place to put my anger and finding strength in knowing
I am true to myself. I took a photo of myself at the bus
depot so I could see myself.

I wish I knew who I was right now.

Sometimes my 'victim self' demands to be seen and gets
lost in the bigger battles for justice. The best hope is that
one of these days the ground will get disgusted enough
just to walk away leaving people with nothing more to
stand on than what they have so bloody well stood for up
to now!

Jaw clenched
I am full of anger
isolated and defenseless
quoting papal encyclicals on the rights of workers
while being told by church leaders to shut up
wanting to silence me again
innocence crucified
agony of betrayal
at the end of my rope
restless
self-destructive.

Is there promise
in compromise?
I am Beyond cynical
morose
depressed
give it a rest.

I cannot deny what I see.
I remember
on a du cœur
what grandma said.
I am warmed and cooled by others
I am nourished by traditions and wisdoms
preserved by many.
If I see farther
it is because I am standing on the shoulders of others.

New Men New Roles

I remember organizing this event to address sex role stereotypes and the systems that create them and reinforce them. The whole system of patriarchy which dominates through unequal opportunity, rewards, and punishments. Internalization of gender roles must be challenged. This was a one-of-a-kind event in 1975, where patriarchy and privilege were examined by men willing to look at themselves.

Exploring institutional sexism in the structure of family, community, church and society. The consequences of what society expects of men. What might real equality look like without patriarchal capitalist power in control?

And so wanting men to do their own work of healing from this system.

I was always a dreamer wanting to vision another way to create healthy nonviolent relations.

Faith and Choice

Organizing yet another event that came out of the need to support Catholic Women's rights to choose. I could not do this work alone, so I provided space to help counsellors support women in their spiritual beliefs. I went to Washington DC to attend a Catholics for Choice gathering of theologians to better arm myself to educate women's centres staff and counsellors about the teachings around free will and choice. A challenging moment to open doors of respect and understanding of women's needs.

Treelogy

(a poem gifted to me while I was sleeping)

Poplar
O sensitive one
no wonder your French name is 'tremble' tree
standing tall and true
quivering at every little bit
of air that touches you
never seeming to stand still
quiet for just one moment
what are you afraid of?

Birches. Birches.
Reaching out
together
yielding easily
swaying freely in the wind
hardly ever alone
always in need
of company
bondage or bonding
which is it really?

Pine. Pine. Pine.
Silently
growing new edges
evergreen
eternal it seems
your wisdom of the seasons
locked away
somewhere
beneath your heavy boughs
giving
stability strength shelter
can you share your mystery?

Letter to Training Native Trainers or TNT

(written by me for those graduating from New Careers in 1975)

Now that you are community leaders, I salute you and honour you.
These questions are now yours to ponder.

How do you help people know the significance of their past?
How do you get them to understand the pathos and beauty of a heritage they have been taught to regard with shame?
How do you help them appreciate their own endurance, creativity, incredible loveliness of spirit? It should have been as simple as handing them each a mirror, but it was not.

How do you show a connection between present and past, when the past is not even past?
What is history anyway? Can people see themselves and their parents and grandparents as part of a living, working, creative movement in time and place?

We need to find ways to tell the stories, to collect them, share them, celebrate them. Ignorance, arrogance, and racism have bloomed as superior knowledge in all too many places of learning.

The work before us now is to change the world. Nothing less or easier than that. It requires a lot of time, mobility, money and a room of one's own – a place where you can think for yourself. Which means heartache and misery and times when you will wonder if independence, freedom of thought, or your own work is worth it all. Believe that it is – that you are making the world better by being real in it. Take the contradictions in your life and wrap them around you like a blanket to keep you warm. Love the questions themselves for they are like locked rooms full of treasure to which your key will fit when you find the door.

Our time together, if nothing else, gave us each other forever. It gave some of us bread, some of us knowledge and pride, and all of us comfort and strength. It broke the patterns, shattered phony promises, renewed our purpose, awakened our dreams and called us to life. Because we live, our time together will never die.

I know you will continue to break the bonds of oppression for yourselves and others until all are free to be, until everyone has taken their rightful place in the Circle. No more, no less.

Thank you again for the life we share with its struggles and joys. Onward and ever.

You've got no excuse now

All you people ever do is complain.
Why don't you get out there and do something?
Stop being such a victim. Things are all free for you.

—Voices around me

Got a voice?
Fight back.
But when you do fight back, they bring in the police or
lock you away in institutions.
A century of institutions will do something to you.
What do doctors know about healing?
What do teachers know about truth?
What do priests know about blessing?
What do social workers know about kinship?

Burnout

I am 40 years old. Weary and bruised from all the struggles. All my adult life has been committed to creating social change and working towards justice in this world, to contribute towards a different future for those after me. In my work as a popular educator, I have been a catalyst for change within organizations and groups who are ready, willing, and able to learn and grow. By this very fact, my work has been mostly with women, youth and Elders and marginalized communities in our society; and not with those who will not share power.

Now it is time to heal my spirit. Gifting myself with a Santa Fe Desert Women's Writing Retreat. The desert is opening my heart and allowing my new path to emerge.

What is this place
of burning
this ever present
light
penetrating
layers of the past
stripping away
old skins
transforming
the desert
of my heart.

What is this place
of change
parched earth
drinking in
the moonlight
releasing blazes of colour
surprising me.

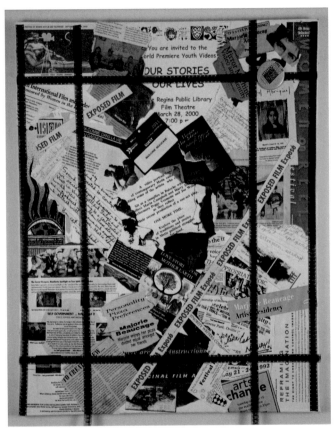

Collage by Marjorie Beaucage. Photo Barbara Reimer.

Story Medicine

(... take care of stories as you would your own children.)

New Love: Cinema

Autumn Equinox: Here I am in Toronto lighting fire, sweetgrass, offering tobacco, and blessing four sacred blue corn seeds from New Mexico to be placed in desert sand and earth. I ask Corn Woman to guide me and fill my dreams and thoughts with creation. I want to make images that embody Light and Vision. I ask these humble little seeds to release their energy so I can learn from them. They are not in their 'natural environment', far from their homeland. I ask them to guide me and help me grow here as I set out on this new path.

Dream: My feet turned upside down like in the womb swimming in new waters of life. Get earthbound feet later. Yellow credits and titles rolling up at my waking: Happy New Year.

I am at Ryerson Film School: industry oriented. Challenging my inner strength and vulnerability of spirit at the same time. I feel alienation and anger at teachers' threats and warnings. Watching films with worldviews that are not mine. Discovering the wonder of cinema and dancing with Light. Will my technical skills match my 'big ideas?' The camera feels like a foreign object in my hands. A horrible sensation. I am learning.

New Moon: Corn plants sprouted! New growth. Two leaves each. I love the drops of water delicately balanced on translucent new greenery. I feel joy.

Hallow Eve

You're in deeper waters... time to give up... time to
give in... tread those deeper waters...
'til the tide brings you in.

—Sylvia Tyson song

Coming to Toronto is a way for me to walk into newness
and celebrate my creation self in wondrously free ways of
being. Knowledge fills yearning and contains assurance in
the fear and tremble of it all. Drawn to transgress my own
boundaries. Trusting.

Circle is cast
thin line between us and ancestors is crossed
stories shared
faces glowing in the candlelight
touching the underbelly of life
tasting the seeds of death and rebirth
our gentle spirits entering deeper into themselves.

Blessed be!

Bingo

When an inner situation is not made conscious,
it appears outside as fate.

—Carl Jung

Excited about this documentary project! No 'talking heads' is the challenge I give myself. Essentially me. Breaking through barriers in every way. Crossing frontiers. To the edge of me, and back again. I am at my best when I do not know. When I can explore from the inside out. I can deepen subjectivity rather than making the story 'objective' or generalize in a didactic manner. 'Emik.' To force out, put out. 'Imik' to penetrate, take in. It is both movements. There is not much new under the sun. Simply different patterns and forms recurring. Perspective is just a way of seeing. Conventions of story forms. Heroes: just another status quo consumer item absorbing the values and struggles and reinforcing dominant norms? Where is the room for difference then? Does anything really change with heroes around? I want to be working in the gaps. What do I want to say in images? Not feeling at home in the film culture around me.

"Women's Dreams Come True" chain letter provides the funding for my first film. Mail comes in every day with money in it, two dollars at a time. I receive $486.00. I believe!

Exploring my own victim mind and programming. Life. It's a game of chance. You play. You win. You lose. Again and again. It's worth the risk. What you risk reveals what you value.

Next time? Is possibility enough? There is no sense in forgetting and every sense in dreaming. Only victims of loss believe. Not enough to go around. Still daring to hope. Longing. Knowing that somehow you win and lose simultaneously. You can feel like a victim and be loved in that secret silent place that seems unreachable. It is 'both/ and' rather than 'either/or.'

It is all about 'having a chance' here. Going deeper and truer. Looking forward to wholeness and balance together. I am committed. Deep bliss. I am a winner. Alive. Bingo!

Story is Medicine

Finished my Renata the potter film with multiple soundtracks. It is one of the best visuals I have made to date. That first image with the foot on the pedal is so me, my professor recognized it right away as my 'signature'! Me: pushing down: deep deep deep, rings of life flowing endlessly, widening and spiraling.

And then that borderline of tired, sad, weary. That female fatigue that comes from loss of contact with one's own being. It is hard to balance on the edge of need for space and need for intimacy. I want more. The flow of maintaining connectedness, of understanding and being understood, of negotiating different needs. Wax and wane. Room for both. Ebb and flow. I want more flow. I don't want to stop. Not be swept away. I need to learn to save a little love for myself. A taste of fullness makes me feel the emptiness so much more. The hurt is real, but it is also calling for healing. Yes. I stand on the border line of my soul with open arms. Waiting. Break apart or break open?

Working on BINGO gives me access to my inner voices, the victim part, and the one who needs more healing. Reclaiming my ground. Solidity. Fear and trembling. Screams and wails. Releasing victimhood.

Learning Steinbeck editing. First rough assembly. Laying down effects track with a bingo dabber's drumbeat. Editing is the search for the film. Breaking down structure and reassembling in new ways. Like a puzzle. Keeping the thread of wanting and showing the machinery of the odds. A music track: choosing the Berlioz Requiem because he broke the rules and had a symphony with quadraphonic sound where convention said no instruments at all. Yes! So perfect. Wonderful feeling. I can create soundscapes! Letting go the exodus scene of losers leaving. Finding a breakthrough point. I am a winner! A dream and some buddies to make a film.... BINGO is in the can!

Artivist Emergence

nothing lights a fire like a dream deferred
—Four the Moment song lyrics

Film shoot at Cape Croker for diabetes film, part of *Sugar Blues* work with Gary Farmer. Gifted with strawberry teaching. And how to make corn soup. Used ashes from a fire to husk chaff off the kernels. Jan Longboat's house is like a little cocoon full of medicines and herbs.

Downtown Alternative School video on peacemaking: "*No Denying.*" I captured their dream on video. They felt affirmed. Youth learning skills and resolving their own conflicts gives me hope for the future.

Native Women's Symposium – Women and Politics: Lee Maracle "I AM WOMAN" speaks of the infinite number of people behind and before you. Maria speaks about art as not separate from history, community, and self. Finding the grandmother in me. Honouring the power of artists to give back through story. Story has power to heal. I am connecting the dots of my life/art/spirituality. All sacred paths.

Evolving my voice and style as I explore telling stories with communities. *Kideo Worxx*. An interactive summer video camp with my friends' kids at my house.

The artivist emerges. Need to create spaces and allies with filmmakers of colour. Needing to have community so I start organizing a series of events to take our place in media since we don't really have one.

Opening doors: organizing events again!
Reel Aboriginal
Race to the Screen
Full Screen
Shooting the System
About Face About Frame

Protectors of Mother Earth: Sagow Aski

From the Toronto jungle to Northern Saskatchewan *Protectors of Mother Earth: Sagow Aski* blockade at Wiggins Bay. At the request of Elders, I arrived here with a borrowed camera from New Initiatives in Film at the NFB. Camera is witness. A feeling of homecoming – tall pines, poplars, white birch, gentle moss, soft sand. And across the way: Clearcut. Mother Earth massacred, ripped open and spilled out.

Waiting for the power to charge the two batteries I have so I can interview the six Elders and the thirty-one who were arrested in the night on Canada Day. 1992. 500 years later – SWAT team escorting logging trucks out. Drying out blankets after rain. Kids hanging around me. Camp meetings. Suzuki visits. Some camp politics exist between clans and areas. Elders are the centre. Some of the guys want to be more militant. Band issues are interfering with elder issues, camp structure and operations. Corporate folks keep talking about 'co-management' plans for the forest – their way of justifying resources they want to just take.

Woodpile is getting low. So is the food. Eating rubber chickens. Lots of Bannock. Huge jackfish arrives. And last night when my tent leaked and my blankets got wet, Mary made me a dry bed in her camper. Adopted little sister she calls me. They are teaching me Cree. I provide the camp entertainment with my accent. Gospel songs on the night air and Ambroise playing his fiddle. What can we do to stop these corporate rapists? And talk of a winter camp, building cabins. A moose came into camp this morning. Food.

The United Church Aboriginal Commission and the Metis Society leaders and Northwest mayors coming to camp for a meeting. The discussion is about how the Canoe Lake meeting was manipulated by Meadow Lake Miller Paper Co. The co-management issue is being defined by NorSask and company. Elders are not part of negotiations. Leaders are selling out for new trucks. The Circle to resolve camp operations (food distribution) and communications helps to change the energy around. The will to continue is renewed. Benefit event will be held in Saskatoon. This Coalition and Elders are not in sync. Solidarity not there. Lots of legal and political stuff to work on.

Over the course of the two years the blockade was up, I went back and forth collecting stories and feelings about what was happening to the People and the Land. It was very discouraging because the government forced them into a catch-22 situation. They took the Elders to court for a million dollars each and then said they would not negotiate anything until they left the blockade. The Elders counter-sued the government for not doing an environmental assessment and then they had to make a choice of continuing with their suit or keeping the blockade. Since the Elders did not trust the courts, they dropped the case although I think they would have won it. In the end, the companies and political leadership sold them out anyway. So, there are no more negotiations or blockade, and everybody has been pretty well bought off. The companies and the government had their way. Still so colonized. It would have been bad news at the best of times.

Access to the tools of production

The artist is the one who can go back and forth beyond the boundaries of cultural agreements and is usually labelled deviant for it. Storytellers transcend boundaries, look back in from the outside and interpret what they see. The images, songs, stories they give back to the people are the bridge between the past and the future.

An oral tradition based on collective experience gets lost in the Western model of culture. Our own interpretations have not been available to us in this dominant world view. The Land, the seasons, rhythms, cosmic time, ceremonies, rituals, stories are now part of re-constructing ourselves. There is a gap in our ability to access our languages, traditional governments, community agreement and the tools we use in this time and place. To de-colonize our minds, our bodies, means to regain our humanity, to re-learn by example, experience, renewal ceremonies, storytelling, praise, recognition. To restore belonging and our sense of place.

What do we mean when we say, "I know?" The future is behind us. Sounding impregnates matter and changes things. Words, language, are representations. Sound is not. It is a vibration, a resonance. The Land herself creates soundings, sends sound signals despite the sound corpses in the universe, all the noise that interferes. It is hard for the spirits to get through. Sound carries Spirit. Our ways are open to the future. There is still room for new revelations, each new day coming to us as the future. Our heritage is not merely a collection of objects and stories from the past, but a complete knowledge system learned through apprenticeship, ceremonies, and practice. Simply recording images, songs and words fails to capture the whole context and meaning. These things are learned through a lifetime of travelling through and being in relation with the Land and all who dwell on this earth. We need to return to that place/space where the spirits accompany us. That is home. Returning to our Mother. Do you enter a place, or do you have the place enter you? Ceremony and ritual create that space for spirit to come in.

On Artist-Run Centres and Racism

We do not have to preserve our traditions.
We allow our traditions to preserve us.

—Leroy Littlebear

So how is it that good people trying to support each other can create such chaos within the artist-run centre movement? Is it fear of loss? Are the centres part of the deliberate perpetuation of the status quo of inequality where race is concerned? A failure to realize the wholeness of difference. Sticking to their strict definitions of art and their rules ensures that other world views cannot be acknowledged. For example, the participatory community-based creation that I do, is not considered 'art.'

In artist-run centres, rules discriminate against other ways of working as an artist. Elitist rules where you are not considered 'professional' if you work in a community-based way. Shared ownership of a story is not allowed. Gotta prove it is yours! Art is not separate from life.

What is at the core of cultural practices? The need for community can also become a trap of exclusion if our goals and values are not aligned. We do need alliances in a climate so threatened by difference. Artist-run centres seem fearful to step up.

In the politics of race and representation, it is easy to lose sight of the storyteller and of the community. Institutions have their own needs and agendas. Reclaiming our ways, our lives, our stories seem so threatening to the cultural industries. This is an opportunity to change the rules and not play their game that has always been stacked against us. We need to acknowledge the gift of our stories and take care of them.

Money for values or value for money? This is the current discourse these days as all the cultural funding bodies restructure to survive the economics of the day. Mainstream arts politics do not address the sense of community that an act of creation or storytelling contributes to the spiritual survival of peoples. Our experiences and the process of coming into relation with our reality through the act of creating is a spiritual one. Giving back what we have received is transformative and renewing; a way of being and doing that connects us to each other and to all Creation.

So, we have nothing to lose. We never had money anyway. But we do have to be vigilant because our stories are already being measured as market value. Appropriation and commodification of culture are not just buzz words anymore. They are our reality.

Self-Government in Art

A human being who has a vision is not able to use the power of it until after they have performed the vision on earth for the People to see.

—Black Elk, Oglala Sioux

As artists it is our responsibility to put forward our visions for others to see. That is the stuff that movements are made of. "*...it is the artists that will bring back our spirits*" is a quote about artists attributed to Louis Riel.

At the founding gathering of a National Alliance of the Aboriginal Filmmakers Symposium *(April 3-6, 1991. Edmonton, Alberta)* we dreamed of Self-government in art. To tell our stories our way. By, for and about us. To rediscover our own structures and paradigms from oral traditions. And develop our own independent resources so we develop on our terms. Not fitting into 'industry' rules and criteria where we must 'sell' ourselves and our stories in their 'narrow markets' where we are seen as non-commercial (systemic racism). Gathering up the ancient struggles and new visions all at once felt like coming home.

That was why the Aboriginal Film and Video Alliance was formed: to remember this energy of creation and restore the place of artists. To create a gathering place, a homeland, where we could remember ourselves. Reclaiming a story that is circular and organic, a world view that is cyclical, self-governing. That is spiritual. An enduring sense of the fluidity of the universe in which we live and grow and change.

To re-imagine and reclaim our ground in the intimate everyday things of creating is to become self-governing. By remembering history, turning to our original teachers: the trees, the animals, the four directions, the truths that were given for life on this land are uncovered. Storytellers have the power to move the spirits of the people toward this remembrance.

We fought
We screamed
We cried
We prayed
We gathered
We created together

We searched for our stories
Our ways
Our faces
Say their names
Those who went before
Those who betrayed our trust
Those who sold out
Those who persevered
Those who continue

Recipe for Self-Governance in Art

Structure in accountability and responsibility.
Add in 12 senior artists from different regions to act as a
working group to carry out decisions.
Stir in for good measure: an Advisory of Elders, Studio I
at NFB, and Banff Centre for the Arts.
Establish a Native Film Development Fund: to control our
own business.
Apply to the CRTC for a southern broadcast license
(before *aptn* came to be).
Reclaim *Pincher Creek Festival* and create our own –
Dreamspeakers.
Develop a distribution partnership with V-Tape.
Give birth to *imaginenative film festival.*

Yield: A space for us.

Runner

If I have the belief that I can do it,
I shall surely acquire the capacity to do it,
even if I may not have it at the beginning.

—Mahatma Gandhi

I have been led to the right paths, friends, meaningful work. I have been blessed many times when I trust this flow, depending on the universe to take care of me. This flow of grace moving me to the right livelihood, companions, destiny.

I was chosen by the national Alliance Gathering of Storytellers and Media to be the *Runner*, a cultural ambassador between Arts institutions and our communities of artists. As tradition has it, the 'runners' were the ones who went ahead to prepare the place and the people for what was to come. My role was to make room for us and our ways of seeing and being and establish links with artists and communities to gather at Banff in a culturally safe place.

As a *Runner* I was always negotiating, making room or protecting our space so we could create together. I was like the bouncer between the institution and the projects; whenever there was a problem I was troubleshooting. When I got to Banff there was one of me and all of them – all the departments and their protocols, so I really had to figure out how Banff worked. The various disciplines didn't talk to each other much though they started to have management meetings when their funding was starting to get cut. But they are all very protective of their little turfs and their disciplines, and their dollars, and their scholarships. I figured that out. The first year we did a series of public service announcements (*PSAs On Self-Government, Talk About It, 1994*) because the Media and Visual Arts section of Banff was the most open to having us.

The Alliance works with existing cultural groups. We negotiated a Banff residency for the Native Theatre School which had been in existence for twenty-five years and still had no funding base unlike the National Theatre School which has always had core funding. Even though every year the Native Theatre School had to apply for project dollars, they still created the Graham Greens and the Gary Farmers and the Tantoo Cardinals. We've never had core funding for any of our arts.

The first winter theatre residency was for senior artists who teach and train new people but don't have time to develop their own methodology or cultural forms in a more disciplined way. Winter was the time when theatre was down, music was down, and Banff didn't have programs. So, I said, "Okay let's put something in each of those programs." Come winter the second year, we had a winter camp with a hundred artists from all the disciplines! Suddenly Banff was ours.

I think change is possible. When you look at situations, you've got to be able to see not just the problems, but the possibilities. If you can spark one little person to act, to stand up, it's worth it. All the work I've done is about change and the possibility of doing it together. My life has been group-centred in that sense, because to work alone is defeating. That's why we started the Aboriginal Film Video Art Alliance. We were all struggling with these things on our own and coming up against closed door after closed door. Your head starts to hurt, bashing doors in or trying to sneak in the back way. So, we decided to help each other in whatever ways we could to keep doing the work in spite of the industry pressures in film and television in particular.

We created the Alliance to protect our stories and lobby for change in policies. It takes a long time to do this. So I started at the Canada Council since there was no door to get in. Just small changes at first, like creating an Indigenous Secretariat with one staff to having our own programs. It took years. And the whole debate around cultural appropriation was brewing in the writers' community in the late seventies and eighties. With a lot of lobbying led by Lenore Keeshig-Tobias and writers of colour, some changes were made in the Writers' Union. Even though Margaret Atwood and Pierre Berton and many others resisted the cultural appropriation issues identified by Indigenous writers, we still managed to have the issues discussed. Those are the battles we still must be vigilant about.

Awakening Our Stories

Once upon a time to come
there were peoples
who knew what they knew
they knew that their heritage on this land was their power
and they knew how to honour
their spiritual connections
with their ancestors.

The women
recovered their powers of creation
in their bodies
in their spirits
in their dreams
and the people remembered
that woman is the medicine
the original power
of earth and moon and stars
and they saw what they might become
and the distant pasts
became one
with the near futures
as stories were shaped
from that ancient place
deep within where the Mother lives.

To go to that place
of remembering
is to be re-membered
sometimes it means
starting with what is
darkest
and wild
and dangerous
uncovering stones

paying homage
to the sacred buried there
sometimes it means
communion
with solitude
to find right relation
and affirmation
of the unloved
self.

And sometimes
a song on the wind
stirred the hearts
of many
and the people
recognized its beauty
in each other
hearts opened
to action
this is how the people
became strong again
because in that moment
was remembrance
and so it continues...

Ntapeu: I am telling the truth

We learn by going where we have to go.
—Rilke

Innu video: *Ntapeu*. I have been asked to help Innu
have a voice and present their research via video to an
environmental assessment panel. The first premise of this
project is that it is community based. It is by Innu, and
they will determine what is to be documented. The second
premise is that by training Innu workers to do the video
research, it will ensure an Innu worldview is represented.
Teach, share, develop voice, and Innu vision. What is
the impact of Mining at Emish, on the land, water, air,
animals, people? What is resource development by Voisey
Bay Nickel Mine doing to Innu life? Community based
participatory research with video is a way for people to
have their voices heard. A document of present reality
that includes the past and the future: a living history.

"What is your ORIGIN story?" I asked. Silence. Someone
replies, "Something about Wolverine." They do not really
know it. Someone else replies, "Heard it a few times
when I was a kid when we were out on the land. I do not
remember it now. We don't go out on the land anymore.
nutshimit – that is where the stories are shared."

"Your first assignment this weekend is to go find it. Ask
the Elders. Record it."

The oldest elder in the community remembered some
of it. In each home is a green screen tv with birthday
messages and music that is playing from an old radio/tv
station in the band office. It is not really staffed or used.
So, we figured out how to hook it up and broadcasted the

story shared with us to each house. About ten minutes later, the door to the band office opens and an old woman walks in saying: "He forgot this...." Next thing you know, everyone is coming to the band office. And together we retrieved and reconstructed the whole Wolverine Story. How do you measure scientifically the loss of this cultural knowledge at the heart of being Innu? It is more than a socio-environmental impact. It is the spiritual/cultural trauma of the rapid destruction of *nutshimit* – life on the Land.

And I get yet another up-close lesson on how evil corporates try to silence chiefs. I am witness to ultimatums, bribes, pressures to settle, and not protest. Overheard in band office:

Chief Katie: You would just have to ask permission of the Elders.

Company Man: How would you like to go to Florida? Take your family to Disneyworld.

Chief Katie: Pause. NO. Not in a week. Not ever.

Company Man: Would $2 million a year for 20 years do it? If you lead the protest, we can't negotiate.

The socio environmental impact study methodology I am using has been trashed by a University of Manitoba sociologist, hired by the Voisey Bay Nickel mine to discredit our work. He said the research was not scientific because we proposed to present findings from an Innu world view. He said we were messianic and had pre-determined the conclusions. As if they don't! This type of research has not been done by the community before, where the people decided the questions for the survey, looking at past, present and future. Now I know I am on the right track!

Pounding surf and winds for two days, mirroring the pressure of the work here. And CBC reporters still asking the wrong questions: "Native people in Labrador have pitched tents in front of bulldozers. We know the general issues, is it money or environment this time?" Totally ignoring Indigenous Rights and Land sovereignty.

My dream is to create choices. Hopefully making this video will offer some healing and acknowledgement of Innu world forging a path to future possibility.

Light in the Dark

Dear Marjorie,
You are amazing. The work you are doing is groundbreaking stuff. Once it is done, the people will have a better chance at a future. Keep holding them up as they struggle to find their way. It takes a lot of courage to move ahead thru the dark.

Remember how hard it was for you to believe in your own creativity. And how Johanna helped you to own it and affirmed you daily. She saw you. So, believe in them now until they can believe too.

Sometimes, you just push too hard wanting so much to feel acknowledged and heard.
You insist on such high standards, because of that conditioning by the church. You tend to set the bar too high, making the price tag too great, setting defeat in motion. All this is another survival mechanism, a defense/protection from abuse. It keeps coming up in different ways. It is so hard to access other parts of self and others when this conditioning has become the norm.

Support the life of the forest floor. That's where all the new seedlings are. So, when obsession strikes, do the next right thing even if it's something small. Life is grounded on many small daily steps and very few large leaps. You are not at the mercy of unseen forces out there. Just see 'what's next?' Respect where you are and where you want to go, working with what you have. Small actions lead to the larger movements.

You are doing the best you can with the light you have to see by in the darkness.

Ease in. Ease up. One moment at a time.

The loss here is loss of control. Unreasonable expectations and pressure to produce. It's their story. You don't have to be super responsible. Where does that pressure come from?

Encouragement. What you lacked. What you can now give.

Collective Memory: Myth Legend Story – Trickster Spirit.

You can't keep a good monster down.

—Movie Poster for *Ghosts of Frankenstein*

Cyborg angels, the new tricksters, echo shortened memory programs to access the present. Being inside a virtual space. Is there an outside? Outer space? Artificial intelligence? A fragile social space. Constructed. De-stabilizing. Virtual spaces seem like non-spaces presented as gathering spaces designing identity. A full virtual land to get lost in! One can actually get lost in unfoundedness and in the void.

Oral tradition is our virtual reality. Accuracy and newness happen in each time and space the story is shared. These allegorical knowledge maps, like dreamtime, are a space of collective intelligence that we can enter.

Memory is what you remember. What you remember is not virtual. Real is what matters. Information must matter, not just live inside the computer where the virtual is privileged. Virtual is no body. No stakes in the material world. Often replacing or erasing gender and race.

It is hard to locate narrative, subject, experiences in this created world. Loss of body. Loss of memory. Segmentation. Virtual reality is death to self, but computers are the immortals here. Ghostlike shimmering sounds to revive the dead! Culturally, how do you get a curve into a grid?

... here are your instructions

*(Chi meegwetch to all the artists for their vision
and to all the grandmothers and grandfathers
who have gone before us in pre-colonial times.)*

In the face of extinguishment
destructive development schemes
environmental degradation of the Land for profit
re-member we have instructions from the Land
and the wisdom of our ancestors.
We can bring the past into the future through our stories.

Another generation continues to create
making meaning
looking to the Elders for wisdom
looking to the Land
holding it in view for healing.

On playing by their rules

I have a collection of rejection letters from CBC and Telefilm using their conceptual frameworks and criteria of: issue driven, character driven, episodic or stand-alone to tell stories, not considering different notions of time, space, and relations. They have no clue. We are not an 'issue to be addressed or solved.' The institutions at the heart of stories and the naming of oppression are lived realities carried within us and are part of the history on this land that needs healing. By refusing our voices, institutions are still in denial of what happened here.

Excerpts read: "Interesting subject no doubt, but a little on the slow side. Scenery is good but needs to be tightened, cut. Varying inflections in 'narrator's' voice would have added some upbeat interest." So to be clear: storytelling in your own voice is not 'narrating.' So our *Rougaroo* and *Pocahontas* features are not meant to be. Producer school is not enough.

'Objectivity' is a western notion that supports a system of judgments and values built on the assumption that 'they' are superior, and they designed a system to prove it, to create norms in relation to the vertical direction of progress and domination.

Difference is as important as originality. It is the variety of meanings and interpretations that make life truthful. There is not just one uni-versal truth, but multi-versal views. Creating story is a way of expressing complex reality and participating in it. Sharing our history and the many realities it can be made into.

Memory is survival. The struggle to be a nation and to recover ourselves is our task. Make history or be history. Motion pictures are meant to move you, moving the soul to see in new ways.

what I know about filmmaking

The first mystery is light
the visible coming into being
light in time and space

Light shining on
the power of authentication
not re-presentation
with edges to look inside
to look beyond the frame
provoking questioning
and constructing meaning

To look and see
to re-discover
to salvage the essence of everything
that overflows the outline
of reality
of what remains within
after the film is over…

Asking questions: a good recipe

*A work of art opens a void, a moment of silence,
a question without an answer, provokes
a breach without reconciliation where the
world is forced to question itself.*

—Foucault: Madness and Civilization

Take some vision
Mixed with imagination
Add the power to make things happen
Manage your state of mind
Go after what you really want
Focus your attention
Let the story unfold the way it wants to
Ask yourself questions that empower you
What shall I create today?
What is this day for?
What am I looking for?
Authority. Where does it come from?
What is my 'acorn' of truth?
What is essentially me?
My destiny.

Art cannot be removed from the heat and friction of
human activity. It demands engagement and the ability to
see through and beyond the image. I am finding my true
North in developing an independent voice, a community-
based storytelling approach. No formulas here. My ego
wants the recognition. I fear I won't make it, so I say:
"I prefer small time to big time."

Playing small does not serve the world. I must let my light shine. Let my dark shine too. I cannot change the game through confrontation. Practicing men's power games only makes me more subject to them. It's no-win. Not sure I can win them over to enlarging the space either. I have my own power to command and control my world.

Storyweavers

First woman is Grandmother Spider
She birthed herself from the dark void
it took a long, long time
for She had nothing to work with
except the power of her own thought

She dreamed her thought into substance
and as soon as She was born
She began to spin and spin
weaving a Sacred Spiral
upon which the universe was born

Marjorie, her parents, her six brothers and five sisters
on her first visit home as Sister Marjorie.
Photo: Family archives.

All My Relations

O painful life. O the life that is not lived!
O what lonely solitude; how incurable.
What shall I do, O God? What shall I do?

—Theresa of Avila

Love is confrontation with the old in new places

400 years ago, Theresa of Avila, this doctor of the church, wrote her own life and story of mysticism so others could learn. To bear witness, to give personal testament is a very old tradition. She looked truthfully and with simplicity at herself and found the lesson she must write about – the lesson of intimacy and divine union.

Finding the place within where we are not divided from our spirit self is a wild journey. There is no path. Love is confrontation with the new. Asking questions. It is response ability. Being in relation to the whole. In so doing, I am seeing my personal history and conditioning, and moving from it. Leaving old ways of responding behind.

Normal was never any good. The battle with doubt and silence fought again and again. Locking myself up. Protecting self at all costs. Struggling to be strong because I am struggling, to be weak because I am. Needing connection and reaching back to make it different for the future. Moving from individual healing to collective change. Bearing witness. Breaking silences. Making new relations with family community. That is what happens as we grow older.

Today I have a mild case of existential blues brought on by this cold that creeps into my very bones. A polar vortex is what they are calling it. The universe is changing. I did not know that the magnetic poles of the Earth attract each other over time and every eleven years or so they actually come so close to each other; they flip! I don't know if these two phenomenon are related but the cold energy is a feminine energy that brings healing. And Mother Earth surely needs it! And if the polar caps are changing too, then maybe the cosmos is asking us to re-balance things. To expand. To not be afraid. This writing is asking me to re-connect myself and feel large, expansive, bold, inventive, creative once again. I have come to know life abides in flux, ever moving, changing, evolving, creating and being created.

Justice. Making things whole. Bringing together the broken bits. Seeking beauty. All works of healing are works of creating beauty. To create is to heal. So I continue making my medicine in everyday things like gardening, kneading bread, writing these reflections.

Echoes and canyons

Too often expectations get in the way of mystery
to leave behind all that is known
searching the heavens
for tomorrow's vision
isn't a risk but a necessity
willing to risk
the kind of involvement
that bares the struggle
of misused ends
and touches the part that hurts
revealing the tangles
that have always been covered
exposing what needs to be brought home

As the sunband and the shadow
move across this spinning stone
spinning us home
we can almost
stride valleys
ford the streams
jump dry rock beds
heeding the cry of eagles
knowing oneness
with the ancestors
singing us home

Desiring Light

We spend our entire adult lives trying to collect the debt owed, to get reparations for an ancient childhood wrong. While we do that, we are also creating a debt for the next generation of children. Accept the childhood loss. We can't fix our parents' sorrows or win the love that was not granted. Walking away from past injustices, choosing to live in the present is power. Give your inner child a hug and give thanks for the light.

I have lived most of my life in groups yet ultimately alone. Always feeling the need to respond, to be available because I have no children of my own. So, I have given myself away. And been taken. Expanding to the breaking point and back again. In light and in darkness. To-ing and fro-ing in the quest for balance. Like an atom dancing in space.

A heart story

*If nature puts a burden on you by making you
different, it also gives you a power.*

—Lame Deer

on a du cœur grandma said.

Yes, I do have heart
lose heart
seek heart
find heart
heart is not a cure for loneliness
just a rhythm
just there
pa-pom-pa-pom-pa-pom
listen to your heart

Voices of my heart silenced so long –
could this little girl survivor and warrior
share the same heart
strong hearted victims
silenced
by heart politic controls?

Protecting protecting protecting
defending sacred space
not to be taken again
so brave and stoic
survivor spirit taking charge
living with unbending purpose
balancing
the terror and wonder
of being human
of being woman

Seeking seeking seeking
for what I did not always know
calling my search truth justice love change
battles exhausting
armour more and more restricting
crack in e-motions breaking open
movements of rage
pain waves of love
tenderness and laughter
pouring over me
tears tearing apart
heart opening
enabling rebirth
making room
laying down my sword and shield

Sometimes
balancing both alone and together
inner and outer
us and them
sometimes knowing
either – or
does not make us whole human beings
to be 'wholly'
living from the heart
take heart

on a du cœur...

Wildflower woman

Woman, you must adorn yourself, dance merrily.
Dance with the noblest loveliest richest queen…
ove wanders about through the senses and
then it storms the soul with all its power.

—Mechtilde of Magdenberg

Free as the wind
uprooted again and again
planted in new gardens
each time different
each time the same
this time
ride the wind
land in your own garden
unleash all your raw beauty
live through storms
let fires burn
survivor is not a calling card
stand knee deep
in the flow of life
pay close attention

Family reunion – making peace

The man who robbed me of my womanhood and
locked me up inside myself for so long, and who denied
responsibility for his actions, now kneels before me asking
for forgiveness. I have wanted to hear those words for so
long: 'I am sorry. I hurt you and caused pain and suffering
through our whole family. I was wrong. Forgive me.'

I am stunned. I accept.
The future is the past healed.
Silence has a new language.
The ground under me has shifted
founding fathers, holy fathers, scientific fathers, biological
fathers,
no longer having power over me.
I am no longer the wounded warrior.

Sylvia – entre les étoiles …

(in remembrance, March 16, 2016)

Sylvia
soul sister
shining star
lifting me up
you got me
in every way
no one knew me like you did
walking together
all our lives
picking blueberries
sharing blankets at folk fest
trading clothes
you
letting life in
all of it
going an extra mile
coming to visit
you knew the road went both ways
I love and respect you
fierce advocate for your kids
cheering them on
every step of the way
so much pride and love
I will always love you.

Good grief

Danny died on the highway. The shock. The finality. The sorrow. Pain. Anger. Closeness. Separateness. All that is left is memory. What was your time here for? Every life has a purpose. What was yours?

I woke up this morning seeing your face on the mountain smiling with the spring rain.

The gift you gave – searching for connectedness through all the family pain. You – bound by the beauty, seeking life's kiss even as death strikes, reminding me through my tears to take care of my heart.

Remembering now.

Family Secrets

Silence.
Locked up.
Protected.
Never naming the depression
that connects us in places
where there is no language
only rivers of silence.
My eyes still leaking fiery hot tears
burden of memory
pressing against me.
Come hell or high water
we stuck together
rancid memories
choke me.

Beatings.
Abuse.
Weeping and praying
no one else gets hurt.
I escaped refusing
to be broken by power
not wanting to remember
shutting down when
it hurt too much to remember.

Ashamed.
Muted.
Practicing forgetting
to survive.
I left my family the pain of silence.
And entered another one.

Am I the last person left
who still prays for you…

Dizaines

I have always been a dreamer. And have made dreams
come true. Creating shared collective dreams is more
challenging. But the ingredients are the same: Passion.
Heart. Commitment. Dizaines was a Metis way of
organizing for battle, ten people to each cohort. So, a
cooperative of Metis artists dreamed a place to create
living history. To make a home for Metis artists in the
Metis homeland at Batoche. To build a contemporary
space with the community. Have a work bee to build a
theatre/stable space and bring back horses. To create a
partnership between artists and Parks Canada. We were
not able to get a memorandum of agreement as we had
hoped for. The shared management board (which included
the Metis Nation of Saskatchewan) would not support our
vision. The Metis Nation of Saskatchewan was wanting
to control the money. When will politicians ever learn to
respect Elders, storytellers, youth, women? This boys club
has got to go! Now is the time for a new leadership. To be
otipemisiwak – a people who own themselves.

Two Spirit Gifts

*My life is for a purpose other than being the head of
some man's lodge. I want to be a friend to all. Look
upon me as a sister.*

—girl chief Medicine Girl

Hello cruel world
time for a little kindness
show some respect for difference
many of us never got to explore sexuality as children
many of us were not taught about our bodies our
responsibilities our roles our gifts
many of us suffered sexual abuse in residential schools
from relatives in our own homes.
No one spoke up for us.

Today I salute this generation
asking for different kinds of relations
needing Two Spirit gifts acknowledged.
mamāhtāwisiwak
spiritual beings
Gifted Ones
wanting rites of passage
ceremonies to take our place
digging through the colonial trash
finding the original blessings
staying alive
rehoming
bringing medicine
balancing masculine and feminine
tastawewiniyak
standing in the middle
healing our communities
making spirit whole.

My prayer: Creator, clean our hearts of any emotional poison that we have. Free our minds from any judgment. That we can live in complete peace and complete love with respect for difference. Open our hearts without fear to share ourselves in freedom to be who we truly are. Rally the love inside each one of us to counter the hate and fear all around, to honour the gifts of Two Spirit.

We know our names best when we are loved.

Space: The Final Frontier

Not just in Star Trek, but in relationships too. The ultimate relationship challenge: space. Balancing desires and longings with inner and outer space. Yin yang is hard to achieve. Space is gravity free. No pulling down force. Yet gravity is the force of attraction. The power that pulls things together. Draws one closer.

And there is something about urgency. About the thirst for life denied, it is deep and fierce. The condition of relationship is not to hesitate, not to hold back, but to pull out all the stops. No room for timidity here. All the weathers. Inner and outer worlds meeting without expectations, to hold to enfold, to give, just because. Yes. Go too far. Off the deep end. To the roots. There, is the prime matter which contains the essence.

Circle

Sharing circles. Holding safe space for stories, for healing. I was twenty-five when I did my first circle with my family. The Christmas after my dad left. Fight was brewing about going to visit him on Boxing Day. Some of us did not want to go. Breaking the silence on sexual abuse is never easy.

We need a safe space where we can open our hearts and minds to each other. According to traditional teachings the circle is that transformative place.

A circle has no sides, no dividing lines to line up on. A circle has no corners to get stuck in, it is open and welcomes all. The circle expands easily to make room for one more. Moving outward, coming in towards the centre and back again.

In the circle each one has their place. No more no less. Each one has a responsibility to speak their own truth, to respect others, to listen to their stories, and learn from each other's experiences.

In the circle there is no right or wrong. No convincing you of my point of view. In the circle my words are not more important than your words because I am older or have letters after my name. The one who casts the circle is the servant of the circle where the intention of the circle is shared and accepted by all who participate in the circle. A sacred trust.

In the circle we experience our connection to all of life. We balance ourselves and re-establish our relationship to ourselves and to each other. That is the law of the Circle of Life. To be united and to be in right relationship, transforming the time and space we share, creating our collective wisdom.

Every time I sit in a circle, I come away enriched and blessed by the shared knowledge and wisdom experienced in community. What makes the circle safe is the protection of the ancestors who assist us. That is why it is important to invite them into our gatherings to ask for their guidance and blessing. It is important to know the keepers of the ancestral memory of the place where we are.

All my relations.

Money money money

Of course it's easy to believe in abundance if you've never known scarcity. Money, or the lack of it, is a recurring theme in my life. I have what I need but I am also living in debt mode. I attempt to change my scripts around money and about worth. I want to win. How should I achieve personal financial independence? It's not chance. I play Publishers Clearing House sweepstakes, lotteries, VLTS, and casino games trying to win and have that moment of what it feels like to live with abundance. It has not happened.

I am most surefooted in those moments when I am true to myself. When doors open and trust triggers the support of the universe. When I am ambivalent and conflicted in my goals my path is that way too. When my intentions and purpose are clear, then life is easier. Let the dough rise. Counting my blessings.

Walking With Our Sisters

"Why are they missing?"

A little girl asks me on the first day. I am a grandmother in the lodge for our missing and murdered sisters. My heart breaks. I don't have an answer for her. What left them unprotected? On their own? Pushed out?

And facing 'protocols' and dress codes. Where did these restrictive rules for Two Spirit and women come from? I have never experienced so much disrespect as I stand to balance what is so wrong. I cannot turn people away for not wearing skirts, for being who they are.

pour que ça change…

Dans les premiers temps d'une relation, qu'est-ce qu'on abandonne? Les scénarios dans ma tête, les mécanismes de survie sont tous en jeu. On entre en relation avec l'espoir de changer, de grandir.

Quand une personne part pour la terre promise
Il faut renoncer aux pays des ténèbres
Il faut quitter les ténèbres et partir pour la lumière
Au-delà des frontières des limitations
Ce sont des vieilles affaires, des vieux vêtements
On ne peut à la fois rester et partir
L'essentiel c'est le commencement.
C'est là que les forces nouvelles se déclenchent et s'orientent.
Le futur est le passé guérit.
Faire la paix avec le passé
Nous réjouir d'être ici maintenant.
Je me laisse emporter
Je me perds dans l'autre
Rêve de promesses en douceur et en harmonie
Je suis dans le courant de ma vie
Ce que l'on cherche, nous trouve
Au cœur du cœur de mon cœur.

Newsflash to my family

Hello! My life is changing changing changing... real fast. I have entered into love and am moving to Quebec with my soul sister. We bought a bed and breakfast, a great old house (circa 1715) with a soul. I am totally happy. Would love to see you here. Anyways, you get the picture. I am moving. I am moved. YES!!

Ancestral Rock, Quebec 2000.
Photo: Personal collection, Marjorie Beaucage.

Wise Fool

*Throughout my whole life, during every minute of it,
the world has been gradually lighting up and blazing
before my eyes until it has come to surround me,
entirely lit up from within.*

—Teilhard de Chardin

Holy Freakness

I am your Holy Freakness.
I came here to be raw and naked.
To burn away the edges of 75 years of conditioning
keeping me from myself.
I came to be a mirror to all your weird and hurting places
because I long for one for mine.
I came to hunt the old stories.
The sly deceits.
The bitter betrayals and fears.
To blast them all to hell and back.
I came to bed down the dark nights of the soul.
To wander into the depths of darkness.
Knowing the dawn will always come.
I came to be messy and get messier
without reactive defense
in the belief that we can disintegrate and mend.
Again and again.

In times of heartache and sorrow I find peace
in stones, in water, in fire.
Where I come from there are songs for tears and dances
for rejoicing.
Where I come from there are also dances and songs for
grief.
There are stones and water and fire.

Hey! Come outside!
The sky is clear.
The wind sweeps you clean.
The sun burns away illusions.
At night, the shadows dance.
Starlight enters.
My eyes open.

From cosmic dust and star song I come
pulled from the fiery bodies of the ancestors
stacked wisdom in my DNA
from cosmic threads untangling Star Self
old forms of self-preservation slipping away
reaching out and back in, arriving from and to
I am stardust on a mission.
I am your holy misfit
birthing elements of creation in the cosmic dance of
justice making
bits of promise dust into us
keeping us engaged with the Mystery of the Ancient Ones
in this stardust soup we are in.
Ancient. Current. Future Matter.
Blended in time wrinkles
bending light.
Creating waves.
Rising from the Black Hole of colonial rule
dancing away in the stuck-ness remembered and
then forgotten.
I have made small stitches back and forth
back and forth back and forth
until the holes in my heart were mended.
A patchwork heart darned in the dark
lit by the stars.

Twinkle twinkle little star...
that is really who you are.
We are stardust
made to navigate the light-ways
to create beyond our reach
into revolution.

I wish I may. I wish I might...

Yes. Now.
The winds of change push us to turn this world around
connect the dots.
Tune in.
The ancestors are live streaming all the time
future memories merging with predictions of the past.
All we need to know is written in the stars.
Listen for star song humming.
Choose consciousness over denial.
Passion over apathy.
Truth over betrayal.
Now is the time.
Our blue Mother needs us.
Waniska!

Catch a falling star!

Poetry of the People

(November 9, 2017, a year after the USA presidential elections)

(Open Mike with Israel Lopez in New Mexico
is a place of new beginnings. Where I read
my poetry out loud. Feeling so vulnerable giving
voice to all that had been kept in silence for so long.
I am ever grateful for this gift in my seventieth
year of life. We are never too old to learn!)

Did you change?
Drop the mike
speak your truth
stories from the heart.

#45 ... make America great???
When a president boasts about deal making skills
big business friends and celebrities as great guys
when a president operates a 'tweet government'
withdraws from the Paris climate accord
approves the Dakota Pipeline and sends in the troops
drops the clean power plan, affordable health care,
women's rights, civil rights, DACA
(deferred action from childhood arrivals)
Saying ME first. I'm number ONE.

I asked my friends
What IS greatness?
My friends say
great is more like small and humble
kindhearted and loving.
Or
considerable

substantial

significant
extraordinary
awe inspiring
magnificent.

I re-member
ancient echoes of stories from long ago.
standing in clearcuts and weeping
witnessing with my camera
the greed and theft of our children's inheritance.
My throat seizing up on the drive through the tar sands
unable to breathe
seeing the black tailings all over the white snow
and an Elders woodpile
sponsored by *petrocan*
What happened to our kinship ties
to the Land
to helping each other
to oral histories
told and retold
to remember who we are?

Waniska!
No twittering away our inheritance
no black snakes cutting thru our waters.
I see people rising rising rising
making their voices heard
Standing Rock solid
protect protect protect
Water is Life
regeneration
generating the future.

New Mexico waters

When I was young
I never knew my attraction to women had a name.
My longings found a home
in women who knew me.
Saw me.
Loved me.
Even if I still did not know how to love my self
my beauty was reflected back to me
That is what love does.

All my relations

I sound the drum
to honour the ancestors of this land
to honour the artists in my equal justice family
who ask the unanswerable questions
who un-cover brokenness
re-connect pieces in new ways
becoming Light Warriors
creating justice
creating stories for the People
honouring our authentic Self.
Weh heh heh…

Grandmother Moon

Grandmother Moon teaches us what we need for the future.
Give yourself permission to change.
What are you passionate about? Do that.
Clear some new paths.
Love your resources, your talents, your gifts.
They will help heal the wound of unworthiness.
Remember gratitude for everything.
Have brutal honesty. What's not working for me?
What burdens am I carrying that are not mine?
Lighten up. Laugh. Celebrate. Affirm. Find your happy place.
What is your source of nourishment?
Your healing power will align with your purpose, your passion, your creative energy.
Connect to what matters most.
Then break it down into small steps.
Decide to give yourself and the people around you the chance to do something new.
A chance to change.
Create a sense of belonging.
Take care of your physical needs to balance health and emotions in what you do.
Stand in your truth.
Take care of this territory that Creator put you on.
The Land knows.
The Land remembers.

if these walls could talk…

Many times I have sat looking at the walls of this log house that is now my dining room, wondering how a whole family lived in this 16' x 16' space, with a porch/woodshed entrance attached. That part was later transformed into a galley kitchen, and I made an old-fashioned pantry for my canning jars.

This part of the house was built by Caroline Dumont, Uncle Gabriel Dumont's niece, 125 years ago. The roughhewn poplar, chinked with mud and red willow are all harvested from the Land around Duck Lake. The house expanded and adapted to accommodate the needs as time went by. The rooms are large for kitchen parties and get-togethers. The community fiddler lived here for fifty years. Laughter and music permeate the walls. So does hardship and 'making do.'

Sixty years ago, when Rose Fleury and her family moved in, a 'living room' was needed so an old farmhouse was hauled in and attached to the one-room log cabin. When I moved in, the living room was like going back in time to the 1970s. It had been decorated with one whole wall of disco mirrors, twelve-inch ones with the gold wiggly lines throughout, wood paneling, shag carpet, a fake fireplace, a chandelier and a front door with glass and brass trim. "Pour faire comme lis riches!" Rose laughed. It was a matriarch's domain, and she took up hammer and nail when changes were needed. I pulled out a bucket full of nails from the walls! Nailed all around the top of every communal room, those nails served for everything from hanging up clothes and medicines to a photo gallery of kids and grandkids and weddings.

An addition of tiny bedrooms and a bathroom were improvised to accommodate the nineteen children who were raised here over the years. Nine of her own and ten others she took in when relatives needed help. Love and laughter seep through the walls to this day. The feeling of comfort and security welcome everyone who comes in. It is a 'lived in' home.

As I write this, I realize that this is the longest I have lived anywhere since I left my homeland in the Sandilands Forest of Manitoba. Twelve years now I've been here. It holds me close. I am welcomed home by the stand of poplars and wild roses, holding time. There are old lady flowers like peonies, hollyhocks, poppies, calendula, lilacs, yarrow and chamomile that have been here forever, attracting bees, hummingbirds and hundreds of dragonflies to take care of mosquitos and pollinate my garden.

I too have made changes to suit my needs. There were just a few tiny windows, probably to keep the heat in. I need light. So I salvaged a large picture window from my neighbour who was upgrading to triple pane for my west facing living room. And Habitat for Humanity windows for the east. Now I enjoy sunsets and sunrises every day. I found an old soaker bathtub at the dump and had it refurbished. I too am following the Metis tradition of 'making do.' My mother re-used and transformed everything too.

Add-ons? Two roofs. Not 'up to code.' Electrical makeshift: extension cords, the old indoor thin one: fire hazards. And now being able to have a woodstove for heat is an insurance nightmare. The well in the cellar was capped by the town. Sask Water decided to put everyone on their chlorinated fluoride system which no one asked for. We've had at least ten boil water advisories in the last year due to frequent power outages that shut the system down or pipes break. This change meant a three-year levy of $180.00 per month on each household because the municipality could not afford this upgrade. It was supposed to be removed after three years. Then we were informed that $106.00 per month was going to be our permanent cost to pay for water and sewage infrastructure. Plus rising fees for the town dump and yearly increases in taxes.

The house needs underpinning support as the dirt walls it sits on crumbled under the extreme weathers we are having. And the exterior paint (Metis blue) is peeling away with time. The house wrap I put on to keep drafts out is now blowing in the wind. My dream to mud and restore the exterior to its traditional Metis style requires skills, labour and resources I do not have.

As a single woman on a fixed income I am having a hard time keeping up financially. Moving into affordable senior housing boxes is not an appealing choice. And selling this house is almost impossible since it would not pass inspection or be approved by banks for a mortgage. Rose and I made a private deal where I could pay for it in instalments. It is in a good location and my fear is that someone would just bulldoze it down and build on the property. This town is famous for destroying heritage buildings.

The seasons of my life are in this place. The changes of the Land around me shape me and inform who I am daily. I have been taught to be resilient and self-sufficient. I was taught by my grandmothers to harvest the Land with respect. Through simple everyday things; not talking about 'culture' but living it. Like out in the blueberry patch when I was seven.

Rose Fleury told me she made a vow to Louis Riel to continue his vision. That purpose is embedded in this house.

Legacy

Between traditions we dance
seeking the higher principles that reconcile.
Story. Ceremony. Relations.
Leaving the solitary prayer cloth dancing in the wind.

Between reason and intuition
between motion and stillness
inhalation and exhalation
stands the Child shaking hands with the Ancestors.
The dust rises into the sky.
In Manitoba, in Duck Lake and at Batoche,
Louis Riel proposed a vision of the world
for which he was called insane
and sent to the gallows.

His vision consisted of equality among the Metis, Indian
and settler peoples. An equality based on the self-
determination of each group in a society based on our
inherent rights. Unfortunately, the government of the day
objected to the idea of Indigenous Peoples as equals and
this grand vision went down in history as a 'rebellion.'
Their ignorance prevented them from seeing the harmony
of plurality and the possibility of justice and human
rights. So under the colonial rule the people could not
share in the power of our cultures. Primarily, Creator
placed us here on this Land as equals. Reality is not what
is. It consists of the many realities which it can be made
into. Look twice to see both the visible and invisible.

Look.
And look again.
It's not about the deal!
It's not about privilege.

It's certainly not about settler privilege
that stole the Land from under us 'fair and square.'
It was there for the taking they said.
This theft, approved by papal decree – terra nullius.
The colonial privilege of having 'final say' on resource
development.
And economic exploitation of Lands and Peoples.
Using police and army, resorting to violence to maintain
the status quo.
The Northwest Mounted Police were brought in
to quelch Metis resisting the theft of their Lands
and protect shareholders' interests of the Canadian Pacific
Railway.
That is the true history of this Land.

COVID 19

Back when the Internet was created, I remember Buffy
Ste-Marie saying how Microsoft systems were first created
as a military machine to kill remotely. And the war
continues as more technologies like G-5 (Huawei) and the
talk of surveillance is seen as necessary.

I remember, as cell phone towers spread across the land,
there were reports of bees being so disoriented by the
vibrations that they were building their combs outside the
hives. The radiation being emitted all over the planet with
the G-5 technology is making us sick and compromising
our immune systems every day.

I remember Bill Gates working to promote big pharma and
HIV cures. And five years ago he predicted this pandemic.
Why didn't he use his billions to prepare for it? Now he is
promoting the vaccine which will be imposed on everyone
so big pharma can make more money.

It's all about energy.
So we need to put out different vibrations
with drum and songs and ceremonies like our ancestors did.
We need to stay strong. Smudge. Sing. Pray.

"We are at war" Trudeau says.
Stay home. Stay safe.
There is so much safety
that safety is becoming the source of danger.
The closed doors of science
looking for a vaccine
that will keep us 'safer.'

Pharmaceuticals and military controlling our movements.
The gun gives way to the syringe.
Go to hell Bill Gates.

Smudge. Sing. Pray.

Three days

Three days.
Three days after being crucified
speaking truth to power
hanging out with the unwanted of the day
you rise up.

Three days.

What's your secret?
Three hundred years and more here!
Still
they crucify
lock us up
medicate
desecrate.

Rise up.
Rise up.
Rise up!

He is risen.
Alleluia!
Magic words.
Alleluia!
Forget suffering.
Alleluia!
Fake happiness.
Alleluia!
Fake righteousness.
Alleluia!

Refusing to wear masks
in the name of Jesus saves.
Alleluia!
No need to be responsible
for each other.
Alleluia!
Bring your guns (to the rally).
Intimidate.
Alleluia!
Kill cuz you're having a bad day.
Alleluia!

Spring uprisings
no longer peaceful protests
Seeking justice
being the changer and the changed
truth is stronger than this fiction of safety
created to keep us apart.

Seeds of hate
will not take root
in this old heart of mine
weary of decades
of stolen privilege
fake power.
Love is stronger than hate.
We will go on
singing our songs.
We shall overcome.

We are rising rising rising
Alleluia!

Spark me PRIDE

Once upon a star there was a time...
a time when the world was dark and needed a little light.
And so it was in the vast secret of the universe
a shimmering quivering fire broke free.

Star gazers often studied the heavens
hoping for a star to shine
revealing mysteries.
Many stars burnt themselves out.
And still longing remained.
Night covered earth once more
and there it was.
Maybe it had been there all along
but no one noticed.
On that special star-filled night
hearts were gladdened, throbbing full.
And everything changed.
And they knew.
But they didn't live happily ever after.
They had to learn to let starlight in
and be starlight for each other.
Again and again and again.

So
take care of your spark
remember your name
walk through the corridors of your heart
you are the storehouse of history
with all its treasures and tatters
search through them for what you need
turn around
reach out

sing their names
names of helpers, ancestors, children, loved ones
until at last your call is echoed
making way for new relations.

Moon Sisters

Sacred Circle
Full Moon rising
Gathering us home
Woman medicine

Every time you display your wisdom out loud
I am granted a space to discover my own
Every time you give context to the struggle of being on
this path
I find my feet on a new walk
Every time you choose to speak your softness
I am made safe
Thank you for staying human
For being the weaver
Thank you for spinning threads from all facets of life
A tapestry of possibility
A beautiful mess
Fabulously flawed
Matter to create our futures
In the places where we rise above the fray of our fear
And just keep going and going and going

2020 senior

in your eyes
I'm a senior
walking this land
living below the poverty line
unseen
unheard
you don't know me
as a strong two-spirit woman
self-governing
part of a people who own themselves
building bridges across difference
asking the hard questions
imagining possibility
creating safe spaces
in which to explore and thrive

I am purple

Soft as lilacs
vulvic deep purple unfolding,
wet yielding surrendering
letting go
I am old lady strong and wise purple
I am royal and ecclesial purple
deserving of dignity and respect
I am grape wine burgundy purple
blueberry centres and saskatoons
to feed the bears and the birds
I am dark and opaque purple full of silent mystery
I am end of the rainbow band purple
offering hope and the promise of never again
I am shade loving pansies and frivolous petunias purple
hardy survivor, constant bloomer
I am grief and mourning purple
awaiting resurrection and joy
I am spiritual chakra purple
allowing light in
opening doors

nipi

Walking on water
remembering
artesian springs under my feet
quenching my thirst
like nothing else

Those waters from home
home waters
threatened now
Greed mongers
no care for life spirit
ever
never
nipi needs us
now

And so I walk
I walk for the river
I walk for the women
I walk for life
I walk for tomorrow

The air so fresh
so crisp
bare naked
truth of why we are here
remembering
finding balance
like this
each step a prayer

I was alone with the trees
and the wind said
breathe
I heard
the song that seeps through the water
songs dreaming into my bones
flaring through memory
dormant songs unsung
dormant songs stuck
I didn't pull away

It was trust
for the dream
that was never lost
for the parts
that spark stars
in the fire
smoke wafting through us
water cleansing
opening into the doorways
opening all the waterways
where we become
a memory
that place where we surrender

Epilogue

Out takes

This is not a memoir full of cool stories and accomplishments. I left out many acts of challenging authority, being called a heretic from the pulpit, changing billboards and hymn books to inclusive language and liberation theology in the middle of the night, co-creating a bakery, a bed and breakfast, health action with participatory research before the term existed, collecting sniff bags in back streets and asking kids what they needed, setting up homes and camps and centres on self-governing principles when the colonial social work welfare model was the only frame of reference, opting out of competency based training for human relations, going out on the Land, bringing Trickster to town, creating an interactive storytelling approach to the Indian Act.

And all those times I hurt myself challenging authorities to make room for difference, speaking truth to power with my uncomfortable rants, going to bed lonely, hungry to be seen and heard. All this and more is the stuff of my life quest for justice.

Moves

Part of my movement in life is change, picking up and going where I need to go.

Countless road trips, camping trips and pilgrimages to Chicago, New York, Cumbermere, Banff, Newfoundland, Santa Fe to renew my spirit. Travels to the Philippines,

Trinidad, China, Hawaii, Virginia, Cuba, California, Switzerland, Paris and the North to explore new places and worldviews. And the thirty places I have made home across this land. All these moves are part of me. I am forever blessed.

Marsii to the Universe for taking care of me and showing me where I must be.

Acknowledgements

All my relations, the ones before me and after me.

My heart is full of gratitude to the ones who carried me through the dark and made fires to warm me, walked with me, guided me. Marsii to my huge extended blood family and the many chosen and adopted ones who supported me. Marsii to Sister Claire, my high school teacher who first believed in me and encouraged me to write. Marsii to all the women who loved me unconditionally and helped me see my worth. Marsii to all my lifelong friends and co-conspirators, C.U.T. mentors and cohorts, AFVAA artists and storytellers, Two Spirit Societies across Turtle Island, and the youth who challenged me and loved me along the way.

Marsii to the Santa Fe Arts Institute and the Equal Justice Residency cohorts with whom I started this journey. Marsii to SK Arts for grants to give me time to write and create. Marsii to Rita Bouvier, editor par excellence, for patiently teaching me about this publishing/writing world; kindly showing me the way around conventions of ellipses, single quotation marks, mid-sentence capitalizations and use of all-CAPs (I did manage to get away with some!) and helping me find the flow of my writing. Marsii to Susan Sacobie for creating such a beautiful cover. And to Kegedonce Press for giving my story a home. With much love and respect, I say Marsii Cho.

Author's Biography

Marjorie Beaucage is a Two-Spirit Métis Auntie, filmmaker, art-ivist and educator, a land protector and a water walker. Born in Vassar, Manitoba, to a large Métis family, Marjorie's life's work has been about creating social change, working to give people the tools for creating possibilities and right relations. She has been a Grandmother for Walking With Our Sisters; the Elder for OUT Saskatoon; and the Elder-In-Residence for the University of Saskatchewan Student Union. As a current Board Member of Chokecherry Studios, she is giving back to future art-ivists as they stand up for themselves and their community through creating art, music, writing. She just finished six short harm-reduction videos for creating possibilities of wellness with story medicine.

Artist's Biography

Susan Sacobie was born in her ancestor's homeland of the Wabanaki people. Susan considers herself a self-taught Indian artist, controversial in its name. Inspiring, vibrant and ever so spiritual in its imagery, her work and life are linked strongly to the universal consciousness which invokes messages and teachings from the spiritual plain. Susan's hope is to share her art and the messages from within the art to awaking mankind's consciousness by using ancient symbols, motifs, imagery and colour.

Susan is humbled to be guided by her ancestors and the ancients. She is obligated to tell and show the world what God and his messengers are teaching her about our connection to the earth, the universe and each other. Despite a tumultuous past that has charmed her earth walk she has survived to paint & dream and to dream & paint. Her mystical wisdom comes from that mysterious place behind the veil and she looks forward into sharing her Indigenous healing art form.

"The purpose for my art is healing & hope, not only for myself but others. It is about being Maliseet, and raising the bar on myself and putting my own unique perspective on Maliseet teachings. It is about pointing out the world's transgressions as well as our own, and reminding ourselves that there is a much higher force guiding and protecting us. Life's events cannot make up our life, and if we stay humble, much like an oyster, we also have the ability to take the metaphorical sands of experiences and events and turn them into pearls of wisdom that must be shared. Colour is life, My aim is to reach past your spirit to your soul and help enlighten not only Maliseets, but the world."